SHINRAN'S
GOSPEL OF
PURE GRACE

MONOGRAPHS OF THE ASSOCIATION FOR ASIAN STUDIES
Published by and available from: The University of Arizona Press
1615 E. Speedway Blvd., Tucson, Arizona 85719

The Association For Asian Studies: Monographs and Papers, No. XX

Delmer M. Brown, Editor

SHINRAN'S GOSPEL OF PURE GRACE

by
ALFRED BLOOM

THE UNIVERSITY OF ARIZONA PRESS
Tucson, Arizona

The original publication of this volume was financed from a revolving fund that initially was established by a generous grant from the Ford Foundation.

Sixth printing 1985

THE UNIVERSITY OF ARIZONA PRESS

I.S.B.N.–0–8165–0405–9
L.C. No. 64–8757

CONTENTS

ACKNOWLEDGMENTS

The author would like to express his gratefulness and appreciation to all those who made this work possible and contributed to its completion. I should like to express my thanks to the Fulbright Commission in Japan for the assistance given during my stay there in 1957-1959. To Professors Ohara Shojitsu, Fujiwara Ryosetsu and Futaba Kenko of the Ryukoku University in Kyoto goes my appreciation for their interest and help in gaining a perspective on the study. To my professors at the Harvard Divinity school who counseled me on the completion of the thesis, Drs. Masatoshi N. Nagatomi, Robert H. L. Slater and Robert N. Bellah go my sincerest thanks. Finally I would give credit to my strongest support through the whole study, my wife, Dorothy Nell, to whom this volume is dedicated.

Alfred Bloom

PROLOGUE

A. Aims of the Study of Shinran's Thought

The central aim of this study of Shinran's thought is to make a systematic presentation of his cardinal ideas which, though well known in general studies of Buddhism, have not been given the detailed attention they merit. It is therefore hoped that this presentation will fill a need in Buddhist studies for a more adequate understanding of Shinran which can become the basis for the consideration of his thought in comparison with similar themes in Christianity or other traditions. We may illustrate the need for such an inquiry from the writing of the Christian theologian Karl Barth in which he notes the similarity of the Pure Land teaching of both Hōnen and Shinran to Christian teaching:

> It is only the "Japanese Protestantism" of Genku and Shinran which calls for serious consideration. When I said that its existence is a providential disposition, I meant that we ought not to be startled even momentarily by the striking parallelism of it to the truth of Christianity, but that we should be grateful for the lesson which it so abundantly and evidently teaches. And the lesson is this: that in its historical form, as a mode of doctrine, life and order, the Christian religion cannot be the one to which the truth belongs, *per se* — not even if that form be the Reformed.[1]

While appearing to make concessions to this form of thought, Barth is finally able to dismiss this expression of religion. However, it is because of the lack of a sufficiently full presentation of Shinran's thought that his significance for Christian theology has not been sufficiently grasped.

A further aim of the study is to bring to light another aspect of Buddhist thought which is important for an understanding of the whole range of Buddhist religious experience, especially in a time when Zen Buddhism has been taken by many as representing the only significant expression of Buddhist religion and insight.

Finally the exposition of Shinran's thought should make it possible to assess his status as a religious thinker in the study of world religions. As the founder of a major religious denomination, the True Sect of the Pure Land, in Japan, his thought naturally commands attention. The basis of his appeal may be

---

[1] Karl Barth, *Church Dogmatics*, trans. G. T. Thomson, Harold Knight (Edinburgh: T & T Clark), I-2, 340-344.

found to a large extent in the new and distinctive form of Buddhist piety which he stimulated by his sole emphasis on faith. His thought reveals him as a person of acute religious sensitivities and intellectual capacity.

While Shinran formulated a religious thought which was especially adaptable to the life of the common man, it should not be supposed that his doctrine was vulgar or naive. Based on his own experiences, Shinran challenged traditional views concerning man's religious existence and destiny with a realistic view of passion-ridden human existence. He brought all his abilities into play in the use of texts, language and modes of interpretation. His proclamation of a religion of pure grace, in which the evil common mortal could experience acceptance by the divine reality while still bound to his passions and unable to perform merit-acquiring practices, revealed that he possessed a first-rate theological mind.

In emphasizing Shinran's thought, we do not mean to ignore the contributions of other important religious leaders of the Kamakura era such as Hōnen, Dōgen and Nichiren. Space, however, does not permit a full comparison of Shinran's thought with that of his contemporaries, because our purpose here is to see his thought against the background of the Pure Land tradition in which he stood. It is safe to say, perhaps, that the essential difference between Shinran and other Buddhist thinkers, of his time or any other time, hinges on the denial of the merit acquisition principle. For Shinran, there was no way in which man could acquire merit which he could direct toward his salvation. Hōnen's Nembutsu practice, Dōgen's Zazen and Nichiren's recitation of the Daimoku (the title of the Lotus Sutra) were all repudiated in principle as self-induced efforts to gain salvation. Thus while each of these important figures contributed significant emphases and experiences to the variegated Japanese Buddhism of Kamakura, they would all stand under the criticism of religious practices (see below pp. 202 ff.) in Shinran's perspective.

The method of our inquiry is largely historical in orientation. Historical analysis appears to be the best method for the exposition of central issues of Shinran's thought because it limits the intrusion of the author's own philosophical or religious standpoint.

In approaching Shinran's specific contributions to the development of Pure Land thought, it will be necessary first of all to survey the general historical development of that tradition. In this connection we shall summarize the basic content of the three Pure Land sutras which are regarded as the sacred texts of the tradition. Following the description of the sutras, we shall give a brief study of the Pure Land teachers whom Shinran regarded as the forerunners and authorities of his own thought. Our concern here will be to trace the orientation of the tradition towards the needs of the common man, and the development of the method of the recitation of the name of Amida Buddha as the means of salvation for common mortals. This study will reveal to us certain inherent problems of Pure Land thought whose solution was given by Shinran's reinterpretation of the doctrine. Some knowledge of the course of the tradition is necessary in order to establish the historical and religious significance of Shinran's teaching.

In connection with our study of the Pure Land tradition we shall also analyze Shinran's concept of this tradition. It is necessary to indicate his theological interest in the tradition in order to have a clear understanding of why he felt justified in reading his insights (perhaps arbitrarily) back into the tradition and thus claiming the support of the patriarchs for his particular views.

In attempting to see how Shinran substantiated his claim that his teaching was the consummation of Mahayana doctrine, we shall limit our discussion to those central doctrines in which Shinran's particular contribution to Pure Land thought becomes clear. It is not our intention here to present the doctrines in the manner of a theological text book. Rather we deal only with those elements specifically influenced by the inner dialectic of Shinran's religious consciousness.

The major doctrines in Shinran's thought which we shall take up are those which describe the human predicament, the nature of faith, the status of the believer, the nature of religious devotion, and the final destiny of the believer. In explicating these concepts we shall depend mainly on Shinran's own words rather than the systems of doctrine arranged by Shinshū theologians. Through a contrast of the traditional conception in each case with his view and method of substantiation, we shall attempt to show clearly where Shinran, on the basis of his own experience and insight, went beyond his teachers in the Pure Land tradition.

Before taking up Shinran's thought directly it may be helpful to summarize the general historical background of his life and the outstanding features of his own life which provide the context for his thought.

B. Summary of the Historical Context of Shinran's Thought.

The immediate context of Shinran's thought was the transition from the Heian age to the Kamakura period which acted as a creative impetus in Japanese culture, not only in the arts but also in religion. Against the background of upheavals and social turmoil of this period, there appeared outstanding Buddhist leaders who attracted considerable followings among the common people. Each in his own way challenged the people of their times to apprehend religious reality within themselves independent of great ceremonies and ecclesiastical institutions. An outstanding characteristic of the preaching of such men as Hōnen, Shinran, Dōgen and Nichiren was their bold attempt individually to discover and declare without equivocation or reserve the one essential truth of Buddhism, as they saw it, required for salvation.

While Shinran's life (1173-1262) transpired against the background of the great changes to which we have alluded above, he was not himself intimately or directly connected with them. Yet it is evident that he was deeply influenced by the spirit of his times so that he has come to be regarded as one of the most outstanding representatives of the spiritual effect of that momentous change in Japanese society.[2]

Although the information we have concerning Shinran's life does not permit us to correlate his teaching more integrally with the stages of his career, it may be useful to provide an outline of his life as merely a general background or context of his thought. There are four established facts which enable us to divide his life into four major periods. Shinran was present on Mount Hiei; he attended Hōnen's hermitage in Yoshimizu in Kyoto; he was exiled to Echigo province and later taught in Kanto region; and finally he returned to Kyoto where he died.

The first period of Shinran's activities on Mount Hiei in the years from 1181 to 1201 witnesses the appearance of religious dissatisfaction. Although this period is described in various traditional sources, our most certain evidence comes from a letter of Eshinni, Shinran's wife, to her daughter Kakushinni where she relates that Shinran became concerned with his future destiny while he acted as a temple priest (Dōsō) on Mount Hiei. She tells of his visit to the Rokkakudo temple in Kyoto where he received a vision which was influential in his renouncing the monkish life of Mount Hiei and entrance into the fellowship of Hōnen.[3]

While it is impossible to determine the psychological or social reasons which led Shinran to reject Mount Hiei and its disciplines, it is possible that he was simply an individual who was constitutionally unsuited for the rigorous practices of meditation in the Tendai system. After years of serious study and sincere attempts to achieve some degree of spiritual insight, he experienced frustration and inner conflict. There are indications that his rejection of Mount Hiei was grounded in a deep sense of sin which must have developed through his years of training. The very nature of his thought shows that it was an attempt to face up positively to his sinful nature. As we shall see, he views the existence of passion in men as a sign of Amida Buddha's mercy and the earnest that salvation is assured. This development is only intelligible on the background of the disillusionment suffered on Mount Hiei.

The second major period in Shinran's career was his attendance in Hōnen's hermitage in Yoshimizu from 1201 to 1207. According to traditional accounts, Shinran made visits to the Rokkakudo and after a mystical experience recorded by Eshinni, he went to visit Hōnen. Eshinni relates that Shinran listened to

[2]Masaharu Anesaki, *The History of Japanese Religion* (London: Kegan, Paul, Trench, Trubner & Co., 1930), 181-182. E. O. Reischauer and John K. Fairbank, *East Asia: The Great Tradition* (Boston: Houghton-Mifflin Co., 1960), 545-546. Wm. Theodore DeBary, *Sources of Japanese Tradition* (New York: Columbia University Press, 1958), 188. 209-211.

[3]*Shinshū Shōgyō Zenshō*, (Kyōto: Kōkyō Shoin, 1953), V, 104, 106. (Hereafter refer. to as *SSZ*)

Hōnen's teaching faithfully and was so attracted by it that he ignored all criticisms, replying that he would accept doom in hell for it since he was already doomed as he was.

With his attendance at Hōnen's hermitage a new era opened up in Shinran's life which we may term the period of discovery. This was perhaps the most decisive and critical time of his career, since his acceptance of Hōnen's teaching marked his rejection of the elaborate disciplinary and philosophic approaches to Buddhist enlightenment on Mount Hiei. It symbolized the rejection of the decadent, aristocratic, confusing religion of the time and his identification with the virile, vital and popular teaching of the Pure Land school which stressed the singlehearted recitation of the name of Amida Buddha. Shinran long remembered the event and in the epilogue of his work *Kyōgyōshinshō* he stated,

> But I Gutoku Shinran, in the year 1201, abandoned the difficult practices and took refuge in the Original Vow.[4]

During this period Shinran made a close study of Pure Land doctrine. Evidence of this endeavor has been found in notes which Shinran appended to Pure Land sutras discovered in the Nishi Honganji storehouse in 1943.[5]

As a result of his penetration of Pure Land teaching, Shinran relates that Hōnen granted him permission to copy the *Senjakushu* and to make a portrait of the master. For Shinran, these gifts marked the high point of his spiritual experience and testified to the close relation he had with Hōnen.[6]

Nevertheless these idyllic years came abruptly to an end when Shinran, together with Hōnen and other disciples, was banished from the capital in 1207. The charge was irreligious behavior on the part of members of the community and was urged by other religious orders. Hōnen was sent to Tosa on Shikoku and Shinran to Kokubu in Echigo.

The period of exile and his subsequent work of evangelism covers the time roughly from 1207 to 1245. This was a time of deepening insight and evangelism. The time in Echigo appears to have been significant in his spiritual development, though we have little information concerning it. He was there from 1207 to about 1212. During the exile he married and began to raise a family. It is possible to conjecture that the insights he received from Hōnen had begun to mature as he faced the problems of establishing a new life and existence in this far off place.

The chief contribution of the period of exile to Shinran's spiritual development was the fact that it brought him face to face with the hard realities of the

[4]*SSZ.,* II, 202.

[5]For discussion of these texts see Murin Kasuka, *Shinran Denne* (Kyoto: Shiseki Kankokai, 1958), 147-150; Zennosuke Tsuji, *Nihon Bukkyoshi, Chuseihen* (Tokyo: Iwanami Shoten, 1944-1955), 402-403; Tomitaro Karasawa, *Bukkyo Kyoiku Shiso no Kenkyu* (Tokyo: Toyokan Publishing Co., 1955), 165-166.

[6]*SSZ,* II, 202-203.

life of the common people which he had not known when he lived apart as a monk. His experience was perhaps even more radical than that of the ordinary peasant because of the painful transition of being thrust out of the pleasant confines of the capital into the rigorous life of the villager. He said of himself: "I am neither priest nor layman." This phrase sums up his basic problem. He had lost priestly privileges in the eyes of the state, but he could not entirely cast aside his religious training and interests because he was now merely a layman. Just as he was a priest without privilege, he was a layman without experience.

It was in this context that Shinran probably came to realize that the common man could attain Buddhist ideals in his ordinary life. It goes far to explain the differences which emerged, and which we shall discuss later, between Hōnen's teaching which he must have learned in Yoshimizu and his own. In this new situation Shinran looked deeply into human nature and became acutely aware of the strength and indispensability of the passions and instincts in the struggle for existence. He could not think with the traditional schools that the life of passion was merely to be cast aside in futile attempts to purify the self. On this basis he rejected the duality of the religious and lay life and took seriously the Buddhist principle "Samsara is Nirvana" as something to be applied concretely in the common life. Existentially and philosophically Shinran merged the secular and religious spheres.

Concerning his family we may simply note that he married Eshinni and had some five or six children of whom five are known to history.

In 1211 Shinran was pardoned along with Hōnen and about two years later he travelled with his family to the Kanto region. It is not entirely clear why he went to Kanto. Religious, political, and social reasons have been adduced. However, perhaps the religious is most significant. Shinran, on the basis of a message recorded in a vision,[7] appears to have seen his destiny in preaching to the people in the east which was newly developing.

During his stay in Kanto, centered in Inada in Hitachi, we can be certain that he enlisted a considerable following. In various sources seventy-four disciples are known. The class origins of these persons were varied and there were a few women. His teaching appears to transcend class distinctions, though some have tried to infer that he was a spokesman for the lower classes. While in Kanto Shinran may have begun to compile his major work, the *Kyōgyōshinshō*, which is a systematic, anthological compilation in which Shinran has brought together from various Pure Land texts passages that illumine his faith. While there are numerous theories concerning its formation, it is safe to say that it is the result of a long process on which no date can be placed. According to tradition, the date for its completion is 1224, a date which appears in the last volume.

---

[7] *SSZ.,* III, 640-641, 662.

The period of evangelism in Kanto was a very productive time. However, after a ministry of some twenty years, Shinran decided for some unknown reason to return to Kyoto to spend his final days.

The return to Kyoto about 1235 and his endeavors thereafter are integral to his total career. Though it is often regarded as a "retirement," this does not mean inactivity. Literary evidences reveal that he changed his mode of teaching, not that he stopped teaching. In terms of the future these were the determinative years because he placed in various forms of writings his essential insights.

During this period Shinran lived modestly, supported by gifts and money from his followers. He carried on studies and enjoyed visits from disciples. He also carried on correspondence with his distant disciples concerning doctrinal questions. Various heresies stemming from influence of other schools or misconceptions of Shinran's own teaching appeared and gave him great concern. In answer to these problems Shinran penned a considerable number of texts or copied some Pure Land texts he considered basic.

His letters particularly reveal his personality and the intimate relations he had with his disciples. He gave kind counsel and was sympathetic to their problems. In his instructions he was humble and tactful, yet firm. It is in these letters that we can observe conditions of persecution by authorities and the disheartening incident in which he was forced to disown his eldest son, Zenran, for an apparent attempt to gain control of the Order by using Shinran's authority. However, the situation is marked by great misunderstanding on all sides. Shinran had to resort to this solution when his own judgment and justice were in question.

With the solution of problems of persecution and dissension in the Order, an air of tranquility enters Shinran's letters. Shinran expresses in these later letters some of his finest insights concerning the status of the believer in this life when he has been assured of his rebirth in the Pure Land through faith.

In his final years Shinran carried on the usual activities of writing and correspondence. He received visits from followers as before. He must have become conscious of his age and aware that death might come at any moment and he grieved over the deaths of those he had known in past years.[8]

In his last days Shinran stayed in the home of his brother, Kaneari, who was a Tendai priest. This residence was at a place called Sanjō Tomi no Kōji. He was also attended by Kakushinni, his daughter. In the very last days Masukata, another son, came, as well as Kenchi and Senshin, disciples from Kantō. The *Denne* narrates briefly the last days of Shinran.

> Towards the latter part of mid-winter in the second year Kocho (1262) the Shōnin showed the symptoms of a slight indisposition, and after that his talk never referred to earthly things, dwelling only on how deeply grateful he was to the

[8] *SSZ.*, II, 664-665.

Buddha; he uttered nothing but the name of Amida, which he constantly repeated. On the twenty-eighth of the same month, at noon, he laid himself on his right side with his head toward the north and his face toward the west; and when at last his recitation of the name of Amida was heard no more, he expired. He was just then completing his ninetieth year.[9]

It is not in the province of this study to inquire into the development of the fellowship after the death of Shinran, except to say that soon after his passing his ashes were placed in a tomb in the Ōtani area in Higashiyama section which belonged to Kakushinni. In time this tomb became the center of devotion and remembrance of Shinran, and those who administered it and the memorial services there became the center of the Honganji sect which united the major body of his followers. The mode of leadership was hereditary which became a distinctive mark of this school. We cannot mention here the problems the succession occasioned, nor the problems arising from those who did not favor this method and who formed the Takada school. They derived their teaching through Shimbutsu and Shōshin who represented a spiritual lineage. In addition, there were many problems relating to the connections of the Shinshū community to the orthodox Pure Land schools in the Middle ages in Japan. It was not until the time of Rennyo, the eighth patriarch (1415-1499) that the Honganji sect emerged as a fully independent group. It continued to develop to the present day when it claims to have some 21,024 temples and 9,046,357 believers comprising the two major branches. It is to be noted there are ten schools tracing their lineage to Shinran.

Finally, though Shinran is a man of yesterday, his thought and faith are of today. In consequence of his spiritual impulse the great complex of Shinshū doctrine and schools have emerged. In the post-war period, Shinshū studies have resumed with greater vigor in an attempt to release the spirit of Shinran into Japanese society in the hope that his idealism and faith will invigorate and contribute to the reconstruction of Japan. Having attempted to survey the life of Shinran in its spiritual quest and spiritual outreach in his own time, we must now turn to an exposition of his thought itself.

[9]*Ibid.*, II, 653. Translation from *Buddhism and Jodo Shinshu*, (San Francisco: Buddhist Churches of America, 1955), 177-178.

I

THE BACKGROUND
OF PURE LAND THOUGHT:
THE SACRED TEXTS OF THE
PURE LAND TRADITION

Out of the many Buddhist sutras of the Mahayana tradition three have become especially revered in the Pure Land school. These sacred texts are the *Muryōjukyō, Amidakyō* and the *Kammuryōjukyō*. In this section we shall summarize the basic content of these sutras and introduce those aspects which assumed great importance in the development of Pure Land teaching.

The *Muryōjukyō*[1] in the Chinese translation attributed to the monk Sanghavarman is the chief text of this tradition. This version of the sutra with its record of forty-eight Vows made by Amida Buddha is the basis for the doctrinal development of popular Pure Land teaching.

The title of the sutra means the teaching of Infinite Life. The sutra relates that on a certain occasion Sakyamuni Buddha was on the Vulture Peak near the city of Rajagriha surrounded by his disciples. Because of the illumined, shining visage of the teacher, the disciple Ananda inquired what was the cause of this evident joy. Thereupon Sakyamuni Buddha narrated the story of the Bodhisattva Dharmakara (Hōzō).

According to this story, the Bodhisattva Hōzō in an infinite time in the past was moved deeply as he observed the sufferings of mortal creatures, and from his pity, he vowed to establish a land of bliss wherein all beings could be freed from their many sufferings and troubles. As a result of this desire, he began to inspect all the vast number of Buddha lands and to select the distinctive feature of each. It was his purpose to establish the most perfect land. Conse-

---

[1]English Translations, *Sacred Books of the East* (Hereafter *SBE*), XLIX, F. Max Muller, (ed.), (London: Oxford University Press, 1894-1927), 1-84. Also Kosho Yamamoto, *Shinshu Seiten* (Honolulu, Hawaii, Hompa Honganji Mission, 1955), 7-73. Japanese, *SSZ.*, I, 1-47.

quently Bodhisattva Hōzō made forty-eight Vows in which he promised that he would achieve his goal or else he would not accept enlightenment. The forty-eight Vows related to the adornments of the land, the nature of the Buddha of that land and the beings who may be born there. Every aspect was covered.

The text narrates that Bodhisattva Hōzō labored for long aeons until he accomplished all his Vows perfectly. Since he fulfilled them completely he is depicted as the Buddha of that land, and has come to be known as Amitabha Buddha (Amida Buddha), i.e., Buddha of Infinite Light, or Amitayus (Mur-yōjubutsu Buddha), i.e., Buddha of Infinite Life.

Knowledge of the way of salvation provided by the work of Amida Buddha has been made known to the people of the present age through Sakyamuni Buddha who is shown in the sutra relating the story.

We have already mentioned that the forty-eight Vows of Amida Buddha became the basis for the popular development of Pure Land thought. Particularly those Vows which declared the nature of the Buddha, the way to salvation, and the future destiny of believers became of paramount importance in the doctrinal systems of later teachers. The most important Vows were the Eleventh, Twelfth, Thirteenth, Eighteenth, Nineteenth, Twentieth and Twenty-Second Vows. We may also add that the Seventeenth Vow became especially important for Shinran. Since we shall have frequent occasion to refer to these Vows, it may be helpful if we quote them here for easy reference.

The Twelfth and Thirteenth Vows deal with the nature of the Buddha. In these Vows, the Bodhisattva Hōzō expresses his intention of achieving such merit that his life and light, which signify his compassion and wisdom respectively, will be infinite in time and space. He will thus be a truly universal Buddha. Accordingly the Vows read:

> (12) If, after my obtaining Buddhahood, my light should be limited and not be able at least to illumine hundreds of thousands of kotis[2] of Buddha-countries, may I not attain the Highest Enlightenment.
> (13) If, after my obtaining Buddhahood, the length of my life should be limited and not be able at least to last for hundreds of thousands of kotis of kalpas, may I not attain the Highest Enlightenment.[3]

The Eighteenth, Nineteenth and Twentieth Vows relate to the methods used in attaining birth into the Pure Land, and they figure prominently in Shinran's thought:

> (18) If, after my obtaining Buddhahood, all beings in the ten quarters should not desire in sincerity and trustfulness to be born in my country, and if they should

---

[2]Soothill and Hodous, *A Dictionary of Chinese Buddhist Terms* (London: Kegan, Paul, Trench, Trubner & Co. Ltd., 1937), 322a. A koti may be an enormous number, either 100,000; 1,000,000; or 10,000,000.

[3]D. T. Suzuki, *A Miscellany of the Shin Teaching of Buddhism* (Kyōto: Shinshū Ōtaniha Shumusho, 1949), 15; *SSZ.*, I, 9.

not be born by only thinking of me for ten times, except those who have committed the five grave offences[4] and those who are abusive of the true Dharma, may I not attain the Highest Enlightenment.

(19) If, after my obtaining Buddhahood, all beings in the ten quarters awakening their thoughts to enlightenment and practising all deeds of merit should cherish the desire in sincerity to be born in my country and if I should not, surrounded by a large company, appear before them at the time of their death, may I not attain the Highest Enlightenment.

(20) If, after my obtaining Buddhahood, all beings in the ten quarters hearing my name should cherish the thought of my country and planting all the roots of merit turn them in sincerity over to being born in my country, and if they should fail in obtaining the result of it, may I not attain the Highest Enlightenment.[5]

We should point out here that in the course of the history of this tradition the Eighteenth Vow came to be regarded as the central Vow. Nevertheless the pattern of religious discipline which grew up represented a composite of the religious ideals expressed in all of them. We shall indicate below how Shinran reinterpreted these Vows in order to overcome contradictory tendencies which he perceived in traditional Pure Land thought.

Important in the formation of Shinran's thought is the Seventeenth Vow which promised that all the Buddhas of every land shall praise the name of Amida Buddha and thus knowledge of his work would become universal and available to beings. The Vow reads:

(17) If, after my obtaining Buddhahood, all the immeasurable Buddhas in the ten quarters do not approvingly proclaim my name, may I not attain the Highest Enlightenment.[6]

The Eleventh and Twenty-Second Vows indicate the ultimate destiny for beings for which the Bodhisattva Hōzō aspired. The Eleventh Vow promises that men will finally attain Nirvana when they are born into the Pure Land. The Twenty-Second Vow declares that the ultimate existence of each being is to fulfill the altruism of a Bodhisattva who, after gaining the qualification for highest enlightenment, strives for the well being and salvation of all other beings. The Vows read respectively:

(11) If those who are born in my country, after my obtaining Buddhahood, should not be definitely settled in the group of the faithful before their entrance into Nirvana, may I not attain the Highest Enlightenment.

(22) If, after my obtaining Buddhahood, all the Bodhisattvas in other Buddha-lands should desire to be born in my country and if they should not be all bound to one birth only, excepting indeed those Bodhisattvas who, because of their original vows to convert all beings, would, fortifying themselves with the armour

---

[4]Soothill and Hodous, *op. cit.*, 128a gives various lists. A list common to Hinayana and Mahayana Buddhism includes: parricide, matricide, killing and arhat, shedding the blood of a Buddha, destroying the harmony of the sangha.

[5]Suzuki, *A Miscellany of the Shin Teaching of Buddhism, op. cit.*, 16. *SSZ.*, I, 9-10.

[6]*Ibid., SSZ.*, I, 9.

of universal salvation, deliver all beings from misery...so that all being might establish themselves in true peerless enlightenment, and further be led on beyond the ordinary stages of Bodhisattvahood, even indeed to the virtues of Samantabhadra, may I not attain the Highest Enlightenment.[7]

Sakyamuni Buddha declares that Bodhisattva Hōzō achieved his aims and as the Vows have been fulfilled, a way of salvation is now open for all beings. He is said to have given the Sutra to his disciples, represented by the Bodhisattva Maitreya (Miroku), and to have urged them to proclaim this teaching to all beings.

The *Amidakyo*[8] in the Chinese translation attributed to Kumarajiva is also of great importance from the practical standpoint in Pure Land tradition. In this sutra Sakyamuni Buddha describes in detail the nature of the Pure Land and he explains the meaning of the name Amida Buddha. He points out that all the Buddhas of every direction praise Amida Buddha and this sutra which tells of him.

The features of the Pure Land and the Buddha portrayed in the text are of the highest spiritual order. Though it is a land of bliss, there is no suggestion of physical pleasure or merely materialistic enjoyment. Everything in the Pure Land is designed to convey the truth of the Buddhist teaching to the believer. This is the source of joy and bliss.

The sutra is short, and it stresses the practice of recitation of the name of Amida Buddha and the sutra. These are the means of spiritual blessing and well being in the world. Consequently this text has been very important in the establishment of the practice of recitation of the name of Amida Buddha as the central discipline of Pure Land teaching. Further the recitation of the sutra itself is a prominent feature in Pure Land religious services. It aids the individual to focus his mind and aspiration on the attainment of birth in the Pure Land through its detailed description of that land.

The *Kammuryōjukyō*,[9] said to have been translated by Kalayashas into Chinese, is the third sacred text of the Pure Land tradition. Its title indicates that it is a book of meditation on the Buddha of Infinite Life, i.e., Muryōjubutsu, Amida Buddha. Its central interest lies in the modes of meditation prescribed by Sakyamuni Buddha in order to gain a vision of Amida Buddha or to be born into the Pure Land.

The occasion of the text was the incident in which Prince Ajatasatru imprisoned his father, King Bimbisara, and Queen Vaidehi in the palace at Rajagriha. As a result of this action King Bimbisara died. The queen was greatly disturbed and oppressed in her spirit and in her mind she yearned to be consoled by the Buddha. Sakyamuni Buddha, though at a distance on the Vul-

[7]*Ibid.*, 16, 17; *SSZ.*, I, 9, 10.

[8]English, Yamamoto, *op. cit.*, 101-106; *SBE*, XLIX, *op. cit.*, 89-106; *SSZ.*, I, 67-72.

[9]*Ibid.*, 74-100; *SBE* XLIX, *op. cit.*, 161-204; *SSZ.*, I, 48-66.

ture Peak outside of Rajagriha, became aware of her plight, and permitting her a vision of the Pure Land, he then instructed her in the ways of meditation by which she would achieve a vision of Amida Buddha and thus be freed from the sorrows of this world.

First of all Sakyamuni Buddha instructed her in thirteen forms of meditation. These meditations lead from a perception of the Pure Land and its various features to a perception of Amida Buddha himself. This series of meditations came to be called the way of the "Settled Mind" which means the mind of meditation. This aspect was especially prominent among the monks devoted to Pure Land teaching in China such as Hui-yuan. They sought birth in the Pure Land through meditations which required a considerable spiritual capacity.[10]

Secondly, Sakyamuni Buddha also outlined three meditations for Queen Vaidehi depicting nine grades of people and their attainments which were correlated with their natures. These grades of beings extended from the highest to the lowest in capacity. He pointed out that even among the lowest grade of being salvation was possible, if an evil person, particularly those who committed the five deadly sins[11] or the ten evil acts,[12] on his death bed would recite the name of Amida Buddha even ten times. One's sins would be cleansed and he could gain birth in the Pure Land. As this passage played a major role in the development of popular Pure Land teaching we shall quote it here.

> Some good friends will then say to him (at his last moment), "Even if thou canst not exercise the remembrance of the Buddha, thou may'st, at least, utter the name, Buddha Amitayus." Let him do so serenely with his voice uninterrupted; let him be continually thinking of the Buddha until he has completed ten times the thought, repeating (the formula), "Adoration to Buddha Amitayus." On the strength of (his merit of) uttering Buddha's name he will during every repetition expiate the sins which involve him in births and deaths during eighty millions of kalpas.[13]

This second division came to be known as the way of the "Dispersed Mind" which held up the way of the pursuit of secular virtue and piety in reciting the name of the Buddha as a way to gain birth into the Pure Land for more ordinary beings. The text concerning the lowest grade of beings was used to support the development of a Pure Land teaching adapted to the needs of the common man.

With an understanding of the basic content of the three major Pure Land

---

[10]Zenryu Tsukamoto, "Buddhism in China and Korea," *Path of the Buddha, op. cit.,* 213. Rene Grousset, *Chinese Art and Culture* (New York: Grove Press, Inc., 1959-61), 143. For a detailed study of Hui-yuan see E. Zurcher, *The Buddhist Conquest of China* (Leiden: E. J. Brill, 1959), 194-195, 204-253. In relation to the Amida cult see 219-223.

[11]See p. 155, note 3.

[12]Soothill and Hodous, *op. cit.,* 50a, lists killing, stealing, adultery, lying, double-tongue, coarse language, filthy language, covetousness, anger and perverted views.

[13]*SBE.,* XLIX, *op. cit.,* 198.

texts, we shall now turn to a survey of the popular development of this doctrine as represented by the seven patriarchs whom Shinran singled out as the basis of his own thought.

II

THE BACKGROUND OF PURE LAND THOUGHT: THE SEVEN PATRIARCHS OF THE PURE LAND TRADITION

Our interest in this section is the historical development of the Pure Land doctrine as the background for Shinran's contribution to that tradition. Our study is concentrated on the seven patriarchs revered by Shinran, though they represent only a few of the Buddhist teachers who wrote on Pure Land themes. Nevertheless, the seven Patriarchs whom we shall consider here each contributed some insight which aided the development of a popular Pure Land doctrine which centered its attention on the salvation of the common mortal in China and Japan. This popular, non-philosophical, Pure Land teaching reached its culmination in the doctrine of Shinran.

The Pure Land tradition as a popular form of Buddhism actually began to develop in China. This is clear from T'an-luan's (476-542 A.D.) exposition, Ojōronchū. However, the selection of two Indian patriarchs, Nagarjuna and Vasubandhu, by Shinran as important teachers in this tradition was dictated by several considerations. In the first place the line of continuity of teaching from Sakyamuni Buddha in India had to be preserved. Nagarjuna was believed to have received teaching directly from the Buddha. Secondly, Nagarjuna had come to be regarded generally as the father of all the major schools of Mahayana Buddhism. Therefore it was naturally accepted that he was the founder of the Pure Land school also by Shinran. Thirdly, Nagarjuna was thought to have written the *Jujubibasharon*, a commentary on the Bodhisattva discipline of the *Kegonkyō*. In this commentary there is a section called *Igyōbon*, "the chapter of the Easy Practice," which was later referred to by T'an-luan for its distinction of difficult and easy practices in Buddhism:

> When I humbly consider the *Jujuron* of the Bodhisattva Nagarjuna, it says that
> when the bodhisattva seeks the stage of non-retrogression, there are two paths.
> One is difficult and one is the easy path. . .[1]

This distinction became fundamental in Pure Land apologetic. Even though
Nagarjuna's doctrine was directed toward the training of Bodhisattvas, i.e.
men of a high degree of spiritual capacity, and bore only a distant relation to
the latter popular Pure Land thought, his authority was appropriated by Shinran. Hence Nagarjuna was given the honor by him of being the first patriarch
in the transmission of the truth of Amida Buddha's Original Vow.

Vasubandhu, the second patriarch, had a more direct relation to the development of Pure Land doctrine, since T'an-luan used his *Jōdoron*, a treatise on the
Muryōjukyō, as the basis for his own formulation of popular Pure Land thought.
He extolled the *Jōdoron* as the "ultimate of the Mahayana and the navigating
wind of non-retrogression."[2] However, Vasubandhu, like Nagarjuna, was concerned chiefly with the training of Bodhisattvas, and he also stood within the
highly philosophic tradition of the Yogacara school. His Pure Land thought
provided only the point of departure for the Chinese patriarchs who adapted
the thought to the life of the common man. While the writings of Nagarjuna
and Vasubandhu have been useful in the formation of Pure Land thought, we
must begin our discussion of the popular development of this tradition with the
study of T'an-luan's thought.

In his commentary on Vasubandhu's treatise T'an-luan introduced several
themes which became the basis for all future developments in Pure Land
thought. He began with the observation that he was living in an age when there
was no Buddha present in the world. In such a period, defiled with the five
stains,[3] practices could be distinguished as difficult or easy. According to
T'an-luan, practices become difficult when they are done in reliance on one's
own effort, but they are easy when the devotees aspire for rebirth in the Pure
Land and recognize the power of Amida Buddha's Vows.

T'an-luan was clearly aware that a great distance of time separated the
people of his age from the Buddha. Nagarjuna and Vasubandhu were the last
of the great Bodhisattvas, and they lived in the age of the "quasi Dharma."[4]
No one could claim now to be a Bodhisattva. Hence T'an-luan directed the
focus of Pure Land thought away from the aspiring Bodhisattvas and good men
and women who had been the objects of Nagarjuna's and Vasubandhu's teaching to the ordinary common mortals of his own age.[5]

[1] *SSZ.*, I, 279.

[2] *Ibid.*

[3] Soothill and Hodous, *op. cit.*, 122a. They are (1) the kalpa (aeon) in decay, (2) egoism, (3) passions and delusions as
desire, anger, stupidity, (4) increase in human suffering; decrease in happiness, (5) human life span shortened to ten
years.

[4] *SSZ.*, I, 281

[5] Ennichi Ōcho, "Ken-i-Shōnin' Theory in Jōdokyō," *Indogaku Bukkyōgaku Kenkyū*, III-2 (6) (March 1955), 617-620.
Shinko Mochizuki, *Jodokyōrishi* (Tōkyō: Jōdokyō Hōsha, 1922), 76-77.

The attainment which Nagarjuna and Vasubandhu thought possible in this world through the practice of the Bodhisattva discipline was distributed by T'an-luan between this world and the future birth in the Pure Land.[6]

T'an-luan's concern for the common mortal was made clear in his discussion relating the Eighteenth Vow of Amida in the *Muryōjukyō* to the passage concerning the lowest grade of being in the *Kammuryōjukyō* in his famous series of questions and answers (Hachibanmondo).[7]

In the first question, it was asked what Vasubandhu had meant when he wrote that he desired to be born in the Land of Bliss with "all beings universally." In reply T'an-luan quoted the text on the perfection of the Eighteenth Vow of Amida Buddha in the *Muryōjukyō*. According to this text, "all beings" who think even once (or one moment) on the Buddha, sincerely and with faith, when they hear the Buddha's name, will be born in that land.[8] He took the position that mediocre mortals must also be included in the phrase "all beings." In order to substantiate his idea, he referred to the *Kammuryōjukyō* where it declares that even people who have committed the most desperate sins can be saved if they recite the name of Amida Buddha ten times. Particularly the sutra mentioned those who committed the five deadly sins and the ten evil acts.[9] By establishing this interpretation of the phrase "all beings" in the Eighteenth Vow perfection text, T'an-luan opened the way for the development of a popular Pure Land tradition.

Once having determined that common mortals could be born into the Pure Land, T'an-luan sought to define the practice by which they could attain the goal. He found his solution again in relating the Eighteenth Vow of the *Muryōjukyō* to the passage on the lowest degree of being in the *Kammuryōjukyō*. The phrase Naishi Junen which means "till ten thoughts" in the *Muryōjukyō* was interpreted in terms of the idea of the *Kammuryōjukyō* that the evil man can be released from his heavy burden of sin by reciting the name of Amida Buddha ten times. The foundation of the practice of recitation of Amida Buddha's name was based on the fact that this practice was the result of the Buddha's aspiration to save beings. Therefore the ultimate cause of the effectiveness of the recitation was Amida Buddha himself, and hence it is possible to speak of "Other Power," or that salvation is attained by reliance on the power of Amida Buddha's Vows. In this way T'an-luan legitimized the simple practice of recitation for the common man.

T'an-luan was, however, deeply impressed by the significance of the name of Amida Buddha. He observed that the name of the sutra was *Muryōjukyō*, i.e., the sutra of Eternal Life. He considered the title of the text denoted the name of the Buddha exalted in the book. Also, in the *Kammuryōjukyō* the name of the Buddha was made the substance of the ten thoughts which were

---

[6]Mochizuki, *op. cit.*, 77-78.
[7]*SSZ.*, I, 307-311.   [8]*Ibid.*, 27.

[9]*Ibid.*, 65. Also see passage above p. 3, note 4 and p. 5, note 12.

designed to enable a common mortal to be born in the Pure Land.[10] He was also influenced in singling out the practice of recitation of the name by the general background of the use of magical names and phrases in India and China.[11] Ryōsetsu Fujiwara in a detailed discussion indicates particularly the Taoist influence in T'an-luan's thought. According to this scholar, it was T'an-luan's merit that he could employ popular forms of thought and yet remain faithful to Buddhist doctrine.[12] From his time the nature of the name and its power played an important part in the development of Pure Land teaching.

The name of Amida Buddha was not only the essence of the sutra, according to T'an-luan, but it embodied all the reality that Amida Buddha stands for. He pointed out that to invoke the name was to identify with what it represents. When this is done, the aspirations of all beings would be fulfilled. In order to explain how the name could have such power, T'an-luan related that it was like a dharani or magical phrase of the *Prajna Paramita*. The power of the name was likened to a Mani gem. Just as the jewel purifies muddy water, so also the name in the minds of men purifies them and causes them to cast aside impure thought. Thinking constantly on the name, sins are cleansed and birth in the Pure Land secured.[13]

An essential feature of T'an-luan's thought is the contrast he drew between self power and Other Power. It is fundamental for Pure Land thought. The Self powered person is that individual who fears that he will be born in one of the three unhappy paths, i.e., the hell of fire, the hell of blood, or the hell of swords.[14] In order to avoid this destiny, that person takes up a discipline and through the practice of meditation and concentration he gains divine powers. The Other Power way is likened to the situation of an inferior individual who could but straddle a donkey to travel through the world. However, when he is taken up in the sky by a Chakravartin, he finds that there are no obstacles to his travel through the four continents.

We can rephrase T'an-luan's view to point out more clearly the fallacy he saw in the self power approach to enlightenment. The self power attitude is based essentially on a dualistic view of reality. The devotee believes that through rigorous practices he can build a bridge to infinity, i.e., to purify himself to the degree that he can attain unity with ultimate reality. Relying on his virtue, he may manifest arrogance and pride. Although he claims to be doing

---

[10]*Ibid.*, 279.

[11]*Ibid.*, 314-315. Also Mochizuki, *op. cit.*, 87-88. E. J. Thomas, *History of Buddhist Thought* (New York: Barnes and Noble, 1933-1951), 186-188, points to the primitive origin of spells and charms in Indian tradition. Hidetomo Kaneoka, "dharani and Nembutsu," *Indogaku Bukkyōgaku Kenkyū*, II-2 (4) (March 1954), 500-502, admits that dharani and Nembutsu have the same background in magical practice. He tries to establish a development from magic to religious practice and to faith. The highest stage of faith, according to him, was achieved by Kakuban of the Shingon school and Shinran in the Pure Land school in Japan.

[12]Ryōsetsu Fujiwara, *Nembutsu Shisō no Kenkyū* (Kyōto: Nagata Bunshoda, 1957), 121-125, 131.

[13]*SSZ.*, I, 328.

[14]Soothill and Hodous, *op. cit.*, 62b.

away with ego-clingings, he is actually cultivating them. The Other Power attitude is based on non-dualism. Through the belief that Amida Buddha has fulfilled his Vows ideally, Pure Land devotees believe that they stand on, or in, infinity and whatever concrete efforts they make to reach the goal are really efforts in which infinity itself participates.

While T'an-luan's view of Other Power had great influence on the future development of Pure Land thought, he believed that any practice could be conceived in terms of Other Power. However, as popular Pure Land thought evolved, and the practice of the recitation of the name of Amida Buddha assumed greater importance, other practices such as meditation came to be regarded as self powered practice and the practice of recitation the discipline of Other Power.

T'an-luan gave a strong impetus to the evolution of the popular Pure Land tradition by his deep concern for the salvation of the common man, his theory of Amida Buddha's Vows, the distinction of self power and Other Power, and the establishment of the practice of recitation of the name of Amida Buddha as a valid practice in itself.

The second patriarch selected by Shinran as his predecessor in the Pure Land tradition in China was Tao-ch'o (562-645). This patriarch had become a student of the Pure Land teaching after he visited the Hsuang chung temple in 609. There he read the text of the monument erected by the people of Shih pi to T'an-luan's memory.[15] The monument praised T'an-luan's devotion in spreading the Pure Land gospel among the common people. Tao-ch'o is said to have been so impressed that he said within himself: "T'an-luan is a great leading light of Buddhism and is far beyond me in insight and understanding. Yet he devoted himself to the path of easy practice." Being converted to Pure Land teaching, Tao-ch'o gained a reputation for lecturing on the *Kammuryōjukyō,* and is said to have repeated the name seventy thousand times a day. His major writing was the *Anrakushū* which is a compilation of texts designed to prove that Pure Land doctrine was the only suitable means of salvation in the degenerate age of the Dharma. He also attempted to answer the criticisms of Pure Land teaching by scholars of other schools.[16]

In general, Tao-ch'o merely handed over T'an-luan's teaching concerning the salvation of the common mortal. He was particularly concerned with the question:

> All sentient beings have the Buddha nature, and each one of them must also surely, throughout the numberless kalpas of past time, have met many Buddhas. How is it then that right down to the present time, they continue in the endless chain of birth and death, and find no escape from the burning building?[17]

[15] Shōjun Taneuchi (ed.), *Shinshū Gaiyō* (Kyōto: Hōzōkan, 1953), 112.

[16] *Buddhism and Jodo Shinshu, op. cit.,* 109. Coates and Ishizuka, *op. cit.,* II, 199-200. Taneuchi, *op. cit.,* 115.

[17] Coates and Ishizuka, *op. cit.,* II, 340. *SSZ.,* I, 410.

The answer which Tao-Ch'o made to this question introduces us to two terms which he employed to distinguish the Pure Land teaching from other paths in Buddhism. According to him, beings have been unable to free themselves from the stream of birth and death, because they have not found the two excellent teachings. These are the Holy Path (Shōdōmon) and the Gate of the Pure Land (Jōdomon).[18] In explaining these two aspects of Buddhism, he pointed out that the Holy Path was difficult for the men of his age. It was particularly so because the age was far removed from the time of the Buddha, and the doctrines of the sages were too abstruse and hard for the puny intellects of that age.

He also distinguished the two paths further on the basis that the Holy Path stands for the discipline of stilling the passions and making progress from the level of a common mortal to that of a sage. The Pure Land gate, according to him, teaches that an individual may be reborn in the Pure Land without the cessation of passion. Once in the Pure Land, the devotee will make the transition to sagehood without any hindrances. In the Holy Path the devotee struggles to gain the fruit of Buddhahood in this life, while in the Pure Land school, the devotee rejects the defiled world and aspires to be born in the Land of Bliss and there to attain Buddhahood.[19]

Tao-ch'o was especially noted for the emphasis he made on the doctrine of the degenerate age of the Dharma. Through his writing Pure Land thought became wedded to this thought. He was attracted by the teaching of the *Daishugatsuzōkyō* in which Sakyamuni Buddha was quoted as saying:

> In the latter days of my Law among the millions upon millions of sentient beings who have practised the austerities of the way, up to the present there is not a single one who has reached the goal. This age belongs to the latter days of the Law and it is full of the five corruptions.[20]

In a more detailed fashion he describes the various periods in the process of decline:

> The first five hundred years after my Nirvana my disciples will be sure of attaining deliverance according to my right Law. The second five hundred they will be sure of attaining *samadhi*; the third five hundred, of reading and reciting the Sutras; the fourth five hundred, of building temples and pagodas; the fifth five hundred, of being at variance with themselves and bringing right Law to ruin.[21]

On the basis of this theory of the decline of Buddhist religion, Tao-ch'o concluded that "it is only through the one gate of the Pure Land alone that men

---

[18]*Ibid.*

[19]Kodo Yasui, *Shinshū Shichisō no Kyōgi Gaiyo* (Kyōto: Hōzōkan, 1952), 147-148.

[20]Coates and Ishizuka, *op. cit.*, II, 340-341.

[21]*Ibid.*, 354. Since it was believed at that time that Buddha entered Nirvana at about 1000 B. C., Tao-ch'o could reason that he lived at the beginning of the fourth period.

can pass to salvation."[22] As a consequence of his understanding, he stressed the method of recitation of the name of Amida Buddha and transformed the passage of the *Kammuryōjukyō* concerning the lowest degree of beings into the form of a Vow of the *Muryōjukyō*:

> If there be one sentient being who has committed sin all through life, and who when he comes to the end of life, repeats my name over ten times in succession, without being born into the Pure Land, may I never obtain perfect knowledge.[23]

The significance of this transformation of the Vow is that it makes clear that the object of the Vow is the salvation of the common mortal.

Possibly the real importance of Tao-ch'o for Pure Land tradition lay not so much in his contributions to the thought of that school, such as the distinction of the Holy Path and the Pure Land gate, or his emphasis on the doctrine of the Last Age. Rather his real significance comes from the fact that he was the teacher of Shan-tao, the third Chinese patriarch who systematized Pure Land thought and brought it to its highest peak of development in China.

Shan-tao (613-681) was born just at the end of the Sui dynasty and the arising of the T'ang. His life spanned the reigns of three T'ang emperors. His residence during his teaching career was in Ch'ang an, the capital. In this period the government greatly favored Buddhism as a unifying factor of the state. With the freedom thus given, many great priests flourished and the organization of Buddhist doctrine gave rise to varying schools of thought.

It is related that Shan-tao left home at an early age and studied in traditional fashion the many texts of Buddhism. At the age of twenty-nine years he met Tao-ch'o and was impressed by his lectures. Adopting the Pure Land teaching, he became an active exponent in the capital.[24] In his career he wrote several important works for the study of Pure Land thought.

Most important among his writings is the famous commentary on the *Kammuryōjukyō* (*Kangyōshijōsho*). It is a work divided into four volumes dealing with the basic teaching of the sutra. The sections of the *Jōzengi* and *Sanzengi* which interpret the various modes of meditation (sixteen) were the most important for the development of Pure Land thought. This text sets forth the recitation of the name of Amida Buddha as the primary means of meditation.[25]

On the background of conflicting views on the nature of birth into the Pure Land, Shan-tao attempted to show that Pure Land teaching was not an inferior path. He contended that the sutra taught that Queen Vaidehi was but a common mortal and symbolized the suffering and desperate condition of existence. The sutra was given for the sake of suffering, evil mortals.

The foundation for Shan-tao's thought was his awareness of evil. This intensified sense of human sinfulness, which was glimpsed in T'an-luan and rooted

---

[22]*Ibid.*, 341.   [24]Taneuchi, *op. cit.*, 119.
[23]*Ibid.*   [25]Yasui, *op. cit.*, 166.

in the theory of the decline of Buddhist religion in Tao-ch'o, was made a con-
stituent aspect of the religious consciousness in Shan-tao. Those who would
aspire to birth in the Pure Land through Amida Buddha's Vows had to believe
sincerely that they were "sinful, lowly persons, eternally involved in error, shut
off from salvation."[26] He also expressed repentance in the *Ojōraisan,* and
pointed out that those individuals who cultivate their good roots for salvation
will destroy all hindrances to it if they repent of their sins in this life no matter
how small the sins. When they do this, they gain deep perception. Worship includes the sincere and reverent confession of sin. The confession described by
Shan-tao declares before all the Buddhas and Bodhisattvas that during one's
many births he has repeatedly murdered or injured beings, and he has robbed
and done unjustly. He has had evil thoughts and deceived others. He has
broken all the precepts and taught others to do likewise. He was pleased when
they followed him in sin. Limitless and numberless are his sins, and only the
Buddha can number them.[27] According to the repentance formulated by Shan-
tao, we can observe that he considered all men as perpetrators of the five deadly
sins and the ten evil acts which characterize the natures of the lowest grade
of beings.

Inspired by his insight into the nature of the common mortal, Shan-tao set
about to organize the principles of Pure Land faith in order to show how the
common man may attain birth in Amida Buddha's Paradise. This organization
is based on the three divisions given in the *Ojōraisan.* They are Anjin which is
termed faith and expressed in the three spiritual attitudes of sincerity, deep
faith, and desire for birth in the Pure Land. Kigyō is the practice based in
Vasubandhu's system of discipline, and Sagō refers to the attitudes or modes in
which the practices are carried out.[28]

Anjin, the first division, means literally "to quiet the heart or mind; to be at
rest."[29] In Pure Land thought it signifies faith and also relates to the mind which
operates in relation to the practices (Kigyō). There are three aspects of Anjin
taught in the sutra, namely, the sincere mind (Shijōshin), the deep mind (Jin-
shin) and the mind which desires birth (into the Pure Land) and transfers merit
for this purpose (Ekōhotsuganshin).[30]

It is significant that Shan-tao placed this definition of faith in the forefront
of Pure Land teaching since these three minds of faith had not been mentioned
by T'an-luan, and they had only been considered to relate to beings of the highest level according to Hui-yuan.[31] It was Shan-tao who first asserted that they
applied to all levels of beings and should there be one lacking that person could
not gain birth in the Pure Land.[32]

[26]*Ibid.,* 534. Quote from Morgan (ed.), *op. cit.,* 216.

[27]*SSZ.,* I, 680-682.

[28]*Ibid.,* 648-651.

[29]Soothill and Hodous, *op. cit.,* 212a.

[30]*SSZ.,* I, 60-61.

[31]Mochizuki, *op. cit.,* 106-107.

[32]*SSZ.,* I, 649.

Though Shan-tao's teaching exhibits a deep concern for the common man and a recognition of his sinful condition, the assertion that the three minds of faith were necessary for the attainment of birth in the Pure Land created a problem for Pure Land thought. He did not indicate how beings who have committed the five deadly sins and the ten evil acts could cultivate those mental attitudes. It would appear that a considerable degree of self effort and mental discipline were required. The firmness of mind for which the devotee was to pray and the modes of practice under the aspect of Sagō[33] indicate that this thought was greatly influenced by considerations based on the strong meditative tradition of Buddhism.[34]

Kigyō which pertains to the various practices which may be used to gain birth in the Pure Land assumes special importance in Shan-tao's thought as he singled out the recitation of the name of Amida Buddha as an independent practice. Not only was it independent, but it became the primary practice with all others as auxiliary.[35] In order to clarify this position, he composed the commentary to the *Kammuryōjukyō*. His exaltation of the mode of recitation becomes clear as he made this the central point of the Eighteenth Vow which he read accordingly:

> As it is said in the *Muryōjukyō:* If, when I become Buddha, all beings are not reborn, as they recite my name even down to ten voicings, may I not gain true enlightenment.[36]

We must conclude our summary of Shan-tao's treatment of Pure Land doctrine and practice by calling attention to his famous parable of the "Two Rivers and the White Path." In this parable he set forth in a telling manner the character of existence of a Pure Land devotee.[37]

The parable teaches that every man is travelling toward the West. The traveller desires to go on a road for a distance of one hundred or a thousand ri. However, on the south is a river of fire and on the north is a river of water. Both rivers are deep and wide. They seem without depth or limit. Just between the two rivers is a white path only four or five inches wide. The path runs from East to West, and is about one hundred steps long. The fire and the water threaten to inundate the path at every point. One can never rest on the path.

There were no people in this desolate place except for many robbers and wild beasts. When the robbers saw the solitary individual, they immediately conspired to kill him. The man, fearful of death, ran toward the West but he saw the great rivers, and thought to himself, "I do not see any banks of the

---

[33]*Ibid.,* 649-651. Coates and Ishizuka, *op. cit.,* III, 410, note 2.

[34]Mochizuki, *op. cit.,* 118-122. *SSZ.,* I, 649-650.

[35]*SSZ.,* I, 537-538.

[36]*Ibid.,* 683.

[37]*Ibid.,* 539-541.

rivers on the North or South. Even though I see the small white path, it is very narrow. The shores of East and West are close together, but how shall I traverse this dangerous path? Yet, if I return, the robbers and the beasts will capture me, and if I avoid the rivers on the North and South, evil beasts and poisonous insects will attack me. And if I take this narrow path, I may fall into one of the two rivers." Speechless with fear, he thought, "If I go back I shall die, if I go forward I shall die. Since there is nothing to do but die, I shall investigate this path and go West." When he had deliberated, he heard a voice from the Eastern shore urging him, "You have already decided, go take this road. You shall not die. If you stay you will die." Then on the Western shore he heard a man calling him, "Come right along with singleheartedness and true thought. I will protect you. Do not fear falling into the rivers of fire and water." Then he heard the thieves calling him back and attempting to arouse doubt in his mind with their shouts that the path is dangerous. He paid no heed to them and went forward singleheartedly on the path. Finally he reached the Western shore and escaped all evils.

We can observe in this parable, Shan-tao's great sensitivity to the condition of the common mortal in this world. The common mortal is a person constantly threatened on all sides. Behind, by thieves, and on either side by his passions. Before him lies the unknown road to liberation. In the midst of this condition the traveller must make a decision. Like Pascal, he has to make a wager. As he stands, all decisions and alternatives appear to have the same result, death. Yet the way leading to the West has not been tried and offers a possibility. As soon as he has determined to try this way, he receives support in his decision from the teaching of Sakyamuni Buddha and the summons of Amida Buddha.

The hearing of the voices after the initial decision to seek the way indicates the process of conversion. There can be no conversion not preceded by a desire for a change in spiritual condition. While this parable may have been devised to illustrate the nature of the desire for birth in the Pure Land, it gives a picture of the mortal condition. The desire for birth is amply depicted. It is the intense determination to pass from the world of woes to the world of bliss and will not be obstructed by the distracting threats of the world of decay.

The parable became a document of first importance in the development of Pure Land thought because it graphically portrayed the actual condition of men in the world and the spiritual alternatives before them. Both Hōnen and Shinran referred to this parable in support of their analysis of the human predicament.

Through his organization of Pure Land doctrine and his parable of the two rivers and white path, Shan-tao became a great influence in the development of the Pure Land tradition in China and later in Japan. It is most significant that he first introduced the principle of selection and rejection which was to be employed so powerfully by Hōnen in Japan. According to this principle, Shan-tao evaluated the various Buddhist practices. Some he accepted and some he rejected. He accepted practices devoted to Amida Buddha alone and rejected all others. Among those devoted to Amida Buddha he stressed the recitation of the name, and declared all others secondary and subsidiary.[38]

While Shan-tao was a creative influence in Pure Land history, we must note that the influence of the meditative approach remained strong. He lacked a concept of absolute Other Power, and his concept of faith is still abstract. However, through his analysis of the aspects of the deep mind, his formulation of acts of repentance, and his parable of the white path, he contributed to the deepening awareness in the Pure Land tradition of the ineradicable sinfulness of the common man. In the process of the simplification of practice in Pure Land tradition, Shan-tao contributed greatly to the establishment of the recitation of the name of Amida Buddha as the single requirement for birth in the Pure Land.

Genshin, the first Japanese Pure Land Patriarch according to Shinran's interpretation, was the abbot of Eshin-in on Mount Hiei and lived during the period 942-1017. He was especially significant in the history of Japanese Pure Land thought through his book the *Ōjōyōshū* (Essentials of Rebirth). This book introduced the thought of Shan-tao in Japan and was instrumental in Hōnen's discovery of Shan-tao and the eventual establishment of the independent school of Pure Land thought in Japan.[39]

Genshin appeared in the glorious world of the Heian period which was then approaching its zenith. It was shortly after Genshin's death that the great Fujiwara Michinaga constructed the golden hall of Hōjōji in 1022 and sometime earlier expanded the Muryōju-in which was dedicated to Amida Buddha whose worship flourished during this period.[40]

Within the context of the increasing devotion of the nobility and populace to the worship of Amida Buddha, Genshin could not fail to examine the beliefs of this aspect of Buddhist doctrine. As a prominent Buddhist scholar he is reputed to have studied Hinayana, Mahayana, exoteric and esoteric doctrines, and is credited with writing some seventy books totalling one hundred fifty volumes.[41] Of all these writings, the *Ōjōyōshū* became the best known and most influential.

The reason for the appeal of the *Ōjōyōshū* lay in the intellectual aestheticism of the Heian age. The world of Heian delighted in the contrasts of light and dark, joy and melancholy, the defiled world and the world of paradise. Thus in the age of peace and splendor, when hardly a cloud of the prospective turmoil was on the horizon, Genshin's portrayal of the glories of heaven and the terrors

---

[38]See Kōshō Fujiwara, "On the Interpretation of the Kammuryojukyo," *Indogaku Bukkyogaku Kenkyū*, II-1 (3) (September 1953), 171-172.

[39]Coates and Ishizuka, *op. cit.*, I, 182-184.

[40]DeVisser, *op. cit.*, I, 342-343. Anesaki, *History of Japanese Religion, op. cit.*, 151.

[41]Taneuchi, *op. cit.*, 127.

of hell enjoyed a great popularity.

In addition to the popular sentiment which was inspired by the horrendous pictures of the suffering of the doomed and the delights of the blessed, the *Ōjōyōshū*, as a literary work, commanded the attention of the age. According to A. K. Reischauer, this book may be compared with the work of Dante.[42] By his vivid accounts of the spheres of hell and the reasons for their existence and the way to ascend to the Pure Land, the *Ōjōyōshū* became the foundation for the success of the Pure Land preachers such as Hōnen and Shinran.[43] We may also note that Genshin did not restrict himself only to the written word, but he made paintings of paradise and the saints.[44] His work gained its enduring value because it represented the faith of a poet, visionary, mystic and artist, a faith which in its brilliant descriptions grasped the imaginations and emotions of the the people of his age and succeeding ages.

Along with Kuya and Ryōnin, both popular Pure Land preachers in the Heian period, Genshin is also important because he took faith in Amida Buddha out of the cloisters and meditation halls and made it accessible to common folk in a way they could easily understand. The basic theme which runs through the *Ōjōyōshū* is the fact that salvation is attainable through the recitation of the Buddha's name for the spiritually weak in the degenerate age of the Dharma. Such a consoling note inevitably appealed to those individuals who could not undertake the rigors of monastic discipline, but yet were prey to all the anxieties and evils of existence. Through his descriptions of the corruptions of existence and the various levels of hells which were the result of evil deeds committed in the past or present life, the devotees would naturally develop a desire for release from the prospect of such a fate. Continuing on in the work, the aspirant would turn his eyes to the contemplation of the glories of the Pure Land. In turn he would be encouraged to take up the practice provided by the Buddha's Vow which could secure his future arrival in the glorious land of bliss.[45] After presenting both the negative side of the defiled world and the positive aspect of the Pure Land, Genshin devoted himself to a discussion of the practice of recitation of the name.[46]

Though Genshin appears in the *Ōjōyōshū* to advocate the simple recitation of the name of Buddha as the way to birth in the Pure Land, in reality Genshin stood for the view that meditation was the superior way and recitation was the inferior way. Genshin was thoroughly schooled in the way of Tendai philosophy and practice. The Tendai conception of Nembutsu, the process of thinking

---

[42] A. K. Reischauer, "Genshin's Ojoyoshu," *Transactions of the Asiatic Society of Japan,* Second Series, Vol. VII (December 1930) 18-19, 20-22.

[43] *Ibid.,* 16-17. Anesaki, *History of Japanese Religion, op. cit.,* 152.

[44] Anesaki, *History of Japanese Religion, op. cit.,* 153. DeVisser, *op. cit.,* 334-336.

[45] Sanson, *Japan: A Short Cultural History, op. cit.,* 244-245.

[46] Coates and Ishizuka, *op. cit.,* II, 194, note 2. A. K. Reischauer, *op. cit.,* 18-19 gives a brief outline, and on 95-97 an outline of chapters 3 to 10.

on the Buddha, taught that the way of recitation was but a subsidiary means to realize the meditative ecstasy by which the devotee could experience the union of existence and nonexistence as taught in Tendai philosophy. It was thought that by gaining a vision of the presence of Amida Buddha, all distracting thoughts would be banished and the mind would be free to attain the highest insight.

Genshin went beyond the traditional Tendai standpoint when he valued the way of meditation and the way of recitation together. He regarded the meditative practices as impossible for the common man and therefore did not require them. However, the way of recitation advocated by Genshin was not the simple recitation later taught by Hōnen. Coates remarks that "Genshin, while emphasizing the efficacy of simple invocation, also taught that the worshipper should be moved by religious aspiration, should ever keep in his mind a picture of the Buddha's majestic form, with a profound faith that it is he who will save us and welcome us to that land of bliss, and with full determination to reach it, keep calling upon his sacred name at all times and under all circumstances."[47] It is clear that the vocal Nembutsu has not attained a completely independent status in Genshin's thought.[48]

Such a view of the recitation of the Buddha's name has led the famous Pure Land scholar Mochizuki to epitomize Genshin's position as the theory in which meditation is superior and recitation is inferior.[49] Despite the fact that he taught the way of recitation, the basis of his teaching was in the Tendai system of meditations in which the recitation was subsidiary.[50] Although Genshin declared that the way of recitation was suitable merely for interior people, his contribution to the development of Pure Land thought is not to be underestimated. Genshin's thought had a great influence on both Hōnen and Shinran. Hōnen had stated that the fundamental truth of the *Ōjōyōshū* lay in its support of the recitation of the name, and he placed Genshin on a level with Shan-tao in the promotion of the sole practice of the recitation of the name.[51]

The most important patriarch for Shinran was perhaps Hōnen, the seventh and last in his interpretation of Pure Land tradition. Hōnen was his revered teacher, and under his guidance, he gained his initial insights into the way of salvation through faith in Amida Buddha. Hōnen was also extremely important in the development of the Pure Land school in Japan, not so much for his doctrinal understandings as for the combination of religious, social and political

---

[47]Coates and Ishizuka, *op. cit.,* I, 38.

[48]Daisetsu Suzuki, *Essays in Zen Buddhism,* Second Series (London: Luzac & Co., 1933), 137-138. See also Yasui, *op. cit.,* 247-248.

[49]Mochizuki, *op. cit.,* 143. Also Shōjitsu Ōhara, *Shinshū Kyōgakushi Kenkyū* (Kyōto: Nagata Bunshodo, 1952), I, 95-96.

[50]*Ibid.,* 174-177.

[51]Matsuno, *Shinran, op. cit.,* 15.

conditions which contributed to his establishing an independent Pure Land school.

Hōnen did not go beyond Shan-tao in the basic exposition of Pure Land thought, as the *Senjakushū* testifies clearly. His basic assertion was that the recitation of the name was the practice established by Amida's Vow, and was given to beings in order to make it possible for common mortals to be saved in the degenerate age of the Dharma. It was the only practice which men should perform. It is significant that Shan-tao had implicitly taught the superiority of the recitation of the name, but his teaching did not create opposition like that which Hōnen faced centuries later. Although he was deeply influenced by Shan-tao, he went beyond Shan-tao's implied superiority of the act of recitation to stress the clear superiority of that practice.

During his lifetime, Hōnen was preoccupied with demonstrating the superiority of the simple practice of recitation over all other practices. However, there were many questions which were left unanswered. These questions were left to his disciples to investigate. We can discern in his teaching certain points at which future discussion would arise.

Hōnen followed Shan-tao in the assertion that the three minds[52] must be present if the act of recitation was to result in birth in the Pure Land. He particularly emphasized that devotees were to avoid insincerity and the superficial religiosity which characterized the Heian society. Yet he declared for those people who were anxious about their salvation that all that was needed was the mere repetition of the name of Amida Buddha.

To the question how the three mental states of sincerity, deep faith and desire for birth were to be aroused in evil beings, Hōnen argued that they arose naturally when one believed in the Vow and recited the name of Amida Buddha. He went so far as to virtually identify these mental states with the recitation itself and maintained that even though a person might not know the terms for these mental states, he possessed them naturally through the recitation of the name.[53]

In order to assure the evil man of salvation, Hōnen compressed all of religious faith and practice into the act of reciting Amida Buddha's name.[54] Because of the supremacy of the practice of recitation, the question naturally arose: How many recitations are necessary to guarantee birth into the Pure Land?

Hōnen followed the teaching of the *Muryōjukyō* and Shan-tao that birth could be achieved by just one recitation or hearing of the name.[55] The Eighteenth Vow itself did not actually specify the number of recitations that must be practiced. The language of the Vow says "Naishi Junen" which can be translated "as many as ten thoughts" or "even to ten thoughts." Such a way of

[52]See above p. 15.

[53]Coates and Ishizuka, *op. cit.*, III, 398, 405-406.

[54]*Ibid.*, 396.

[55]*SSZ.*, I, 24, 543.

speaking can be construed as meaning either a lesser or a greater number. Shan-tao had taught that to gain birth in the Pure Land only one recitation was necessary (the lesser aspect), while, however, he also urged devotees to practice the recitation continuously throughout life.[56]

Hōnen, like Shan-tao, urged his followers to continue the practice for one's entire life. He pointed out, however, that those who only do it once may give rise to doubts in their minds about their eventual birth, while those who practice it continuously may do it from doubt in the efficacy of the recitation which would mean doubt about the power of Buddha's name. In this way Hōnen tried to bridge the gap between these two points of view.[57]

It must be pointed out that Hōnen tended to favor the principle of continuous recitation for disciplinary purposes. Without such a discipline, he felt, the religious life would become amorphous and doubts and anxieties would crowd in.[58]

Although Hōnen declared that birth into the Pure Land could be attained through one recitation or through many, and preferably many, there still lay an unsolved problem at the heart of Pure Land doctrine. This is the question: How can it be known that salvation is assured? In the Nineteenth Vow it is pointed out that the Buddha will come to meet his devotees at the moment of their death. This was taken to mean that the devotee had to cultivate the right state of mind in approaching the point of death so that he could perceive the Buddha. Considerable anxiety was aroused as believers strove to keep the thought of the Buddha before them and to cultivate the clarity of mind to see the Buddha. The importance of the last moment in determining the destiny of the Pure Land believer was graphically stated by Hōnen:

> Even though through the days and years of life, you have piled up much merit by the practice of the *Nembutsu,* if at the time of death you come under the spell of some evil, and at the end give way to an evil heart, and lose the power of faith in the practice of the *Nembutsu,* it means that you lose that birth into the Pure Land immediately after death.[59]

It appears from this statement that whatever efficacy the recitation of the name has it is neither permanent, nor necessarily cumulative and lasting. The problem of an untimely death or the possibility that one might not be in the possession of his right mind at the moment of death was a problem for Pure Land teachers. In view of this anxiety Hōnen advised his followers:

> Sometimes a man dies from being choked by his food when taking a meal. Now I say, call upon the sacred name every time you chew your food and swallow it.[60]

---

[56] *Ibid.,* 457, 538.

[57] Coates and Ishizuka, *op. cit.,* III, 395.

[58] *Ibid.,* 426, 441, 531.

[59] *Ibid.,* 407.

[60] *Ibid.,* 396.

In contrast to the uncertainty which was implicit in this thought, Hōnen also taught that "there is power enough in the Nembutsu, even if pronounced but once, to destroy all the sins whose effects have persisted through eighty billions of kalpas. And so you ought to bear in mind that Amida has the power to come forth to welcome to his land those oppressed by the very worst *karma,* and you ought to believe that by simply calling upon his name you will be born there, quite irrespective of whether you have merit inherited from former lives or not, and no matter whether your sins be light or heavy."[61]

The power and virtue resident in the name of Amida Buddha as conceived by Hōnen and the Pure Land tradition should provide assurance of salvation in the present life. However, the name was the practice, and the practice was to be carried out by finite individuals with varying mental states. It can readily be seen that there were many chance elements in this view of salvation and emphasis on practice. In large part, the effectiveness of the practice depended on what the devotee put into it. Consequently the practice of the recitation was in actuality dependent upon self power, the resolve of the individual to gain salvation for himself.

In order to overcome the anxiety in confronting the approach of the moment of death and the prospect of eternal doom, Hōnen and other Pure Land teachers stressed the multiple recitation of the name in order to keep the mind focused on the goal of union with Amida Buddha and birth in the Pure Land.

Our study of Hōnen's thought on the recitation of the name of Amida Buddha indicates that he did not advance that thought essentially beyond that of Shan-tao. It was Hōnen's service to the growth of popular Pure Land thought to make it clear, once and for all, that the practice of recitation was the only practice which resulted in birth in the Pure Land. He raised the practice of recitation from the status of an inferior or subsidiary practice, to the superior practice. While he made the practice of recitation the central practice of his religious discipline, his concept of its nature and effectiveness had not advanced beyond that of Shan-tao or Genshin. Although Hōnen would be the first to deny that he was teaching a doctrine of self power, it does appear that to conceive the practice of recitation as a merit-producing act reflects the self power attitude implicit in traditional Buddhist discipline. Such an attitude is seen in the statement of Hōnen.

> In life I pile up merit by the practice of the Nembutsu, and at death I go to the Pure Land. Whatever befalls, I have made up my mind not to be anxious about myself, and so, come life, come death, nothing troubles me.[62]

It is clear in Hōnen's thought that the practice of recitation is the primary cause for birth in the Pure Land.

---

[61]*Ibid.,* 433.   [62]*Ibid.,* 400; also 430.

Apart from the problems involved in his thought, it was a welcome message to his age. His strong personality and convictions made Pure Land doctrine a beacon light for many weary souls such as Shinran who struggled to find a spiritual haven.

Shinran's Concept of the Pure Land Tradition

We turn now from a historical inquiry into the development of the Pure Land tradition to a study of Shinran's conception of that tradition. In our historical study we have observed the emergence of the distinctive features as well as the problems that make up its history and provide an understanding for the significance of Shinran's thought. However, for Shinran himself, a theological interest in the tradition outweighed any historical consideration as to how the tradition may have taken form.

In view of the salvation which Shinran believed he had received from Amida Buddha, he always viewed his role as a teacher as one of receiving the teaching and of transmitting it to others. He constantly maintained that he only handed on the true teaching of the patriarchs and particularly that of his revered master Hōnen. His exposition of the teaching of the patriarchs was intended simply to express his own gratitude and joy for the benefits that he had received from their teaching.

It is the poem entitled *Shōshinnembutsuge* which appears at the end of the volume on practice in the *Kyōgyōshinshō* in which Shinran's theological interest is made most clear. In this poem he depicted the progress of the tradition as it originated in the mind of Amida Buddha as his concern for sentient beings and was expressed in his Vows designed for their salvation. Through the teaching of the great sage Sakyamuni Buddha the teaching was believed to have appeared in history. This historical transmission was forwarded by the seven patriarchs, Nagarjuna and Vasubandhu in India, T'an-luan, Tao-ch'o, Shan-tao of China, and Genshin and Hōnen in Japan. Thus, according to Shinran, Pure Land teaching proceeded from the eternal, compassionate mind of Amida Buddha, appeared in history and spanned three countries, India, China and Japan.[63]

Shinran's intention in depicting the progress of the tradition through the seven patriarchs was to indicate the single line of truth which made salvation possible to men in this degenerate age. The purpose of all the teachers of the tradition was to point to Amida Buddha's Vows.[64] According to Shinran, the tradition itself is really an extension in the historical world of Amida Buddha's Vows, particularly the Seventeenth and Eighteenth Vows. The Seventeenth Vow promises that Amida Buddha's name will be heard throughout the universe, and salvation will thereby be universally available. The Eighteenth Vow, as interpreted by Shinran, declares that faith is the only true way to salvation. As the historical expression of these transcendental, cosmic realities, the tra-

---

[63]*SSZ.*, II, 43-46; DeBary, *op. cit.*, 212-216.   [64]DeBary, *op. cit.*, 214.

dition has an authority which no individual can claim as his own. Like all other individuals, Shinran is just a hearer, a believer, a follower. He declared that he had no disciples of his own, and in his final words in this poem he declares that his followers should place their faith in the great teachers through whom the truth has come. He does not call for them to follow him.[65]

From the transcendental viewpoint there has really been no transmission. All of the teachers in the tradition are viewed by Shinran as Bodhisattvas, or incarnations of Amida Buddha. As such, they can all be considered as the Bodhisattvas who have returned to this world in order to seek the salvation of all beings. While the transmission proceeds through individuals on the historical level, the tradition as understood by Shinran, should not be treated from the historical perspective alone. In his view the patriarchs do not create the tradition of Pure Land doctrine, but they appear within the tradition.[66] Most important to Shinran was the unity of the doctrine through all the ages because it was based on the Buddha's intention. The transmission from this standpoint can be likened to the passing of water from cup to cup without the loss of a drop. As one Shinshū textbook states:

> Therefore our faith has its origin in the mind of the Tathagata and is transmitted by the good teachers themselves through the ages. Putting it in another way, we may say that the faith of Shinran Shōnin itself is the faith of the seven patriarchs, and the faith of the seven patriarchs itself is the teaching of Sakyamuni. Sakyamuni's teaching itself is the teaching-summons of the great and merciful call of Amida Buddha.[67]

It was his deep and all-pervasive reverence for the eternal and universal tradition of Amida Buddha's Vow which gave meaning and import to Shinran's belief that the Pure Land doctrine was the ultimate teaching of the Mahayana stream of Buddhism. It was this faith which caused him to declare vigorously that he had no disciples,[68] or to refuse to take back sacred texts on which he had inscribed his name from errant disciples.[69] The basis for these acts was the sincere belief that the teaching was not his own, but that he had received it from Amida Buddha through the patriarchs. Therefore all disciples were really those of Amida Buddha, not of Shinran.

Shinran's deep theological interest in the Pure Land tradition prevented him from dealing with it historically as we presently understand historical investigation. The *Shōshinnembutsuge* and the *Kōsōwasan*, an expanded poetical account of the tradition,[70] were primarily theological documents. While noting the specific contributions of each patriarch, he was primarily concerned with the one truth of salvation through Amida Buddha's Vow.

---

[65]*Ibid.*, 216.
[66]Daiei Kaneko, *Shōshinge Kōkoku* (Kyōto: Zenninsha, 1949), 182-184.
[67]Taneuchi, *op. cit.*, 97-98. *SSZ.*, II, 774.

[68]*SSZ.*, II, 776.
[69]*Ibid.*, III, 9.
[70]*Ibid.*, II, 501-515.

Conclusion on the Study of the Tradition
of the Seven Patriarchs

Based on the teachings of the three Pure Land sutras, the development of the Pure Land tradition in China and Japan was one of continual popularization. The Pure Land patriarchs whom we have surveyed all had an interest in making salvation available to the common man who was barred by his social situation from entering into the rigorous monastic life. T'an-luan was particularly noted for his concern for the common man. Hōnen and Shinran also showed great sympathy for the evil common man.

As the common man became the central object of religious teaching, it was necessary to modify the disciplines to suit the needs of ordinary folk. T'an-luan suggested the recitation of the name of Amida Buddha as an appropriate means to gain birth in the Pure Land. Tao-ch'o defended this practice as suitable particularly for beings in the degenerate age of the Dharma. He left the implication, however, that the way of meditation was superior, but merely not suitable for the present age. Shan-tao emphasized the vocal recitation of the name of Amida Buddha. Hōnen followed him and made more absolute his assertion of the superiority of the recitation of the name. Shinran went beyond the whole tradition in emphasizing the aspect of faith and reserving the practice of recitation for the expression of gratitude. Whatever the perspective taken by the Pure Land teachers, they were all motivated by a desire to make Amida Buddha's aspiration for universal salvation a reality in the world.

While the practice of the recitation of the name increasingly came to be the central practice of the Pure Land school, insufficient attention was paid to the relationship of the devotee's spiritual attitude and the practice itself. From T'an-luan to Hōnen, the practice was regarded as a *means for acquiring the necessary merit to gain birth* in the Pure Land. The devotee could view his practice as his own effort to attain it, albeit the practice was given by Amida Buddha and rooted in Other Power. At the heart of Pure Land faith there was a mixture of the conceptions of self power and Other Power. The practice as established by Amida Buddha is Other Power, because its ultimate effect is dependent on the virtue of Amida Buddha's name resident in the formula. However, the recitation depends on the volition of the devotee, else the virtue of the name could never be realized. In addition, the three mental attitudes which Shan-tao stressed had to be cultivated by the devotee to validate his recitation. Therefore, in the tradition before Shinran there was an implicit reliance on self in the attainment of salvation. He declared for the first time in the Pure Land tradition a clear understanding of absolute Other Power and the implications of this perspective for faith and practice.

III

THE HUMAN PREDICAMENT

Our study of Shinran's religious understanding must begin with his concept of the evil beings in the world of the degenerate age of the Dharma. It is in this world that passion-ridden beings are encountered, where Shinran encountered himself, and became aware of the ineradicable sinfulness and desperate character of sentient existence. He employed all of the traditional terms to express his concept of the human predicament. He recognized the passions. He saw man chained by lust, hatred and delusion. He characterized existence as life within the burning house which is the figure most prominent in Buddhist descriptions of sentient existence.[1] The most graphic portrayal of this condition which Shinran undoubtedly knew can be found in the *Hokkekyō*.[2] The analysis of existence as based in the passions and ignorance goes back to Gautama himself who saw that the cause of all evils lay in the human heart.[3] In almost any Buddhist text one will find the description of existence as one of grasping, passion, desire, attachment and ignorance.[4]

This analysis of the existence of sentient beings as passion-ridden became a prominent part of the Pure Land tradition and furnished the basis for the relaxation of religious requirements which we find there. Further, this concept was intensified by the idea of the degenerate age of the Dharma. As the Pure Land teaching became more and more prominent, Amidist teaching gradually won out over all other forms of doctrine promising a blessed after-life such as the Miroku worship which had earlier been strong in China and Japan. The insight was already present in early Pure Land teaching that beings were inescapably evil and needed the help of the Buddha to escape this bondage.

---

[1] *The Saddharma-Pundarika* (H. Kern, trans.) *Sacred Books of the East*, F. Max Muller (ed.), (Oxford: Clarendon Press, 1884), XXI, 72-79.

[2] *Ibid.*, 47-48, 54, 133.

[3] C. H. Hamilton, *Buddhism* (New York: Liberal Arts Press, 1952), 28-32, 40-41.

[4] A similar view is attributed to Kōbō Daishi in Coates and Ishizuka, *op. cit.*, III, 431-432.

The interesting aspect of the development of the concept of man in Buddhism is the fact that the analysis of beings' passion-ridden condition presented in earlier forms of Buddhism was calculated to stir a desire in individuals to transcend that evil and attain enlightenment as Buddha had done himself. Thus the analysis was intended to encourage a person to take up the discipline, purify his spirit and gather merit in order to be released from the stream of births and deaths, or to realize the essential Buddha nature which lay potentially within him. As Pure Land teaching developed, with assistance from the concept of the degenerate age of the Dharma, the function of the concept of degenerate beings reversed itself. Instead of encouraging individuals to rigorous disciplines, the concept indicated that such activities were futile and unnecessary. Because man was so evil, no discipline could avail for him to gain enlightenment on his own. He had to rely on the power of Amida Buddha to achieve it.

We note in Hōnen and also in Shinran interesting uses of the fact that Pure Land teaching had become a part of the teaching of other schools. On the one hand, traditional schools objected to the prominence gained by Pure Land teaching and argued that they also were teaching devotion to Amida Buddha together with the other traditional practices of Buddhism. They stressed the fact that devotion to Amida Buddha did not require the abandonment of traditional disciplines. To this argument Hōnen replied that the fact that such Buddhists felt it necessary to include Amida worship in their systems showed that their disciplines were inadequate to gain enlightenment of themselves because of the depravity of the age. Therefore, it was necessary to rely on the worship of Amida Buddha. However, Hōnen objected to this worship of Amida Buddha by the Holy Path schools because it was merely a secondary aspect of their teaching. The popularity of Pure Land teaching came to be regarded as evidence of the essential truth of its position and as evidence of the futility of the traditional disciplines.[5]

Shinran, as a Pure Land convert, accepted these basic positions. His contribution to the understanding of the human condition comes in the fact that his own experience of futility was a powerful element in the formation of his theology. Throughout his writings we find abundant evidences of his awareness of personal involvement in passions and lust. His personal confessions which expose his sinfulness have given his writings a depth and attractiveness because he has indicated clearly his own identification with the human situation and his teachings are a testimony to his faith that he had discovered the solution to man's eternal problem, himself. Thus we find him lamenting sorrowfully in a poem:

> Even though I take refuge in the Jōdo Shinshū,[6]
> It is difficult to have a mind of truth.

---

[5]*Ibid.*, 348. Also *SSZ.*, II, 786-787.   [6]True Sect of the Pure Land.

I am false and untrue,
And without the least purity of mind.

We men in our outward forms
Display wisdom, goodness and purity.
Since greed, anger, evil and deceit are frequent,
We are filled with naught but flattery.

With our evil natures hard to subdue,
Our minds are like asps and scorpions.
As the practice of virtue is mixed poison,
We call it false, vain practice.[7]

In the midst of this theological writing Shinran confesses his temptation at being regarded a teacher, and that even as a teacher urging men to desire birth in the Pure Land, he is still attached to passions and does not really yearn to go there himself:

I know truly how sad it is that I, Gutoku Shinran, am drowned in the broad sea of lust and wander confusedly in the great mountain of fame. I do not rejoice that I have entered the company of the truly assured; I do not enjoy (the fact) that I am approaching the realization of the true attainment. O how shameful, pitiful![8]

Because Shinran was so deeply aware of his own spiritual condition as a passion-ridden creature, he was very sympathetic with his disciples and other people who found it difficult to arouse enthusiasm for a distant land of bliss or a desire to leave the realm of the tangible and the known.[9]

Further, as the sign and symbol of his involvement with the passions, Shinran adopted the term Gutoku as his surname. This term has the meaning of "foolish, bald-headed old man," and it signified the debased condition of Shinran's life. It became the symbol for that inner attitude of the recognition of one's sinful condition which was aptly expressed in the words attributed to Shinran in the *Shujishō:*

This self who is unable to distinguish right from wrong, good from evil, who has no claim even for little deeds of love and compassion, and yet who is willing just for name and gain to pose as teacher (how shameful!).[10]

Because Shinran was acutely aware of his own passion-ridden nature, he realized that there was nothing he could do to purify his spirit sufficiently to gain the insight and assurance of enlightenment prescribed in the traditional schools, and he drew the conclusion ultimately that no practice whatsoever

---

[7] *SSZ.*, II, 527.

[8] *Ibid.*, 80.

[9] *Ibid.*, 777-778.

[10] Suzuki, *Miscellany on the Shin Teaching of Buddhism, op. cit.*, 140

could assure him of this salvation.[11] It is true that he first accepted Hōnen's solution that the recitation of the name was the easy path given to evil beings for attaining birth in the Pure Land and he was willing to stake his life on it.[12] However, in the course of his religious development, he had occasion to think deeply on the process of the acquisition of merit which underlay all Buddhist disciplines, even that of reciting the name of Amida Buddha. What attracted him was the attitude of the devotees who engaged in the performances of religious exercises. To him it seemed that these individuals believed that somehow they were doing a good act and that this good act was the basis of their salvation. He perceived that such persons were in error from two points of view. On the one hand they failed to take seriously the depravity of beings, and on the other hand, they did not recognize the true meaning of the need for Buddha's assistance in attaining salvation.

As to the essential depravity of finite natures, Shinran came to the conclusion that it was entirely impossible for a person to do a good act. Whatever good deed he appeared to do on the finite level was still evil, because it was done with a calculation in mind and was ultimately intended to redound to his benefit. Thus all good deeds performed by individuals were seen as essentially self-centered and involved in the entire web of passion.

From the aspect of Amida Buddha, good deeds were also considered impossible, because the standard of comparison was Amida Buddha. He had practiced through long aeons of time without the slightest tinge of selfishness or insincerity in order to make it possible for men to be reborn into the Pure Land. He was absolute, incomparable goodness and purity. Shinran appears to have experienced the sense of the Holy in his awareness of Amida Buddha's compassion, and this led him to draw a line between the nature of depraved beings and the nature of the Buddha, so wide the gulf that men could never hope to bridge it with petty good deeds. For Shinran, counter to the general tradition in Buddhism, Amida Buddha ceased to be merely an example or pattern whom one might imitate; he was the high and great inimitable absolute who was the source of salvation. There was no basis for comparison between beings and Amida Buddha, nor any possibility of imitating him. From this standpoint, it can readily be seen that religiously there can be no such thing as a "good deed." All deeds done religiously are absolutely evil and do not contribute to the achievement of salvation as understood by Shinran.

Shinran's rejection of all Buddhist practices which were motivated by a desire to accomplish some good effect was so categorical that he was even led to reject the time honored and traditional ways of filial piety which he set aside on the basis that as a common mortal, he had no virtue within him which could benefit his beloved departed.[13] He also appeared to take an anti-social attitude

[11] *SSZ.*, II, 528.   [13] *Ibid.*, 776.
[12] *Ibid.*, 774.

when he contrasted the compassion taught in the Holy Path in which ethical activity contributes toward ultimate realization of Buddha nature, and Pure Land compassion where a person seeks first to become a Buddha and then may contribute to the welfare of beings perfectly. Shinran again merely pointed to the weakness of the common mortal to perform an absolutely good deed on his own power.[14]

As to the misunderstanding of Buddhists concerning the nature of the Buddha's assistance in attaining salvation, Shinran was very clear. *He shifted the attention away from practices to attitude.* There was no practice whatsoever which a sentient being can perform which would bring salvation. This was true also of the practice of the recitation of the name of Amida Buddha, the standard practice of the Pure Land school. The reason was that the performance of any practice was still spawned in the web of passion and self-seeking. It always had an ulterior motivation, i.e., to save oneself. This concern for self was a mark of the attachment and delusion of beings concerning their essential natures. Shinran went further than the traditional Pure Land doctrine which had concentrated on the practice of recitation. According to the Pure Land school, as the name of the Vow indicates, Nembutsu-Ōjōgan, the Vow of birth through Nembutsu, the Eighteenth Vow was made by Buddha to grant devotees the way of recitation, the easy practice. This practice was easy enough for depraved beings to perform and the name of Amida Buddha within the practice was the guarantee of its effect. In the recitation, the name acted to cleanse from sins and karma and thus make it possible for beings to arrive at the Pure Land and ultimately enlightenment. There was much talk about faith in Amida Buddha's name, or Vow, etc. But basically that faith was directed toward the practice, and it was the practice which brought salvation and not the faith. Thus Hōnen stated his position as Nembutsuihon, "the Nembutsu is the cause (foundation or origin)." Amida Buddha's assistance was regarded as only the guaranteeing of the effectiveness of the name which was the essence of the practice.

Shinran's vivid sense of spiritual incapacity in himself, caused him to see in the Vow the aspect of faith, the spiritual attitude to be possessed by the devotee. He realized that as the practice of recitation may have been given by the Buddha, so also the traits of mind that are necessary on the part of the believer were also given by the Buddha. Thus he made the *act of faith itself the essential basis of salvation,* and the *act of faith was not made by the individual, but by the Buddha in that person.* In this way Shinran designed to remove all self-calculating aspects from religion. He established a religious theory of Buddha's assistance which made every aspect of religion derive

[14]*Ibid.,* 775.

ultimately from the Buddha himself. The Buddha's assistance was not restricted merely to the aspect of practice in the vocalizing of the name of Amida Buddha, but it was expanded to correspond to the act of faith in which the urge to repeat the name was engendered.

Through his own inner experience and his reflection on Buddhist doctrine Shinran came to the conclusion that his destiny and that of all other beings would be to fall into hell were it not for the grace of Amida Buddha and his Vows. We should perhaps let Shinran speak for himself as he declares that good and evil men all stand in need of Amida Buddha's compassion:

> The idea is: however good a man may be, he is incapable, with all his deeds of goodness, of effecting his rebirth in Amida's Land of Recompense. Much less so with bad men. Except for the three (or four) evil paths of existence, where else can their evil deeds bear fruit? Being so, good deeds are of no effect and evil deeds of no hindrance as regards rebirth. Even the rebirth of good men is impossible without being helped by Amida's specific Vow issuing from his great love and compassion which are not at all of this world.[15]

One of the clearest results of the intense awareness of sin which Shinran exhibits is the religious logic in which the deeper and more absolute the involvement of mortals is in passions and sins, the greater is the need for an absolute power to release them from it, since they cannot release themselves. Hence the deepening of the idea of man which we find in his thought was accompanied by a more absolute and objective concept of Amida Buddha and the Pure Land.[16] Nowhere shall we find a better example of this change in perspective than in Shinran's interpretation of Shan-tao's passage on the three mental attitudes.

According to this passage in the *Kammuryōjukyō*,[17] it is clear that in order for the recitation practice to be effective, the devotee must reproduce in himself the sincerity, faith and aspiration which Amida Buddha (as Hōzō) had cultivated when he practiced the austerities which established the Pure Land and the way of salvation for all beings.

Shan-tao, and Hōnen after him, regarded Amida Buddha as the pattern or standard for the religious faith and activity of the devotee. Nevertheless Shinran, as a result of his own experience, could not accept this understanding and he devised an interpretation consistent with his own insight. This interpretation is shown in his interpretation of Shan-tao's statements when he applied the Japanese method of reading the Chinese text.

According to Shan-tao, the devotee "must not manifest the appearance of wisdom, goodness, and purity externally and embrace vanity and falsehood

[15] Suzuki, *Miscellany on the Shin Teaching of Buddhism, op. cit.,* 142.

[16] Ienaga, *Chūsei Bukkyō Shisōshi Kenkyū, op. cit.,* 36-39.

[17] *Sacred Books of the East,* XLIX, *op. cit.,* 188. Coates and Ishizuka, *op. cit.,* IV, 414-415.

internally."[18] Hōnen followed this view when he declared in the *Ōjōtaiyōsho:*

> That which is called "a most sincere heart" means a genuine and true heart, which in turn means that one's actions, words and thoughts are without pretence, and in accord with, and an expression of, reality.[19]

Shinran interpreted Shan-tao's passage differently:

> Do not manifest the appearance of wisdom, goodness and purity externally, *because* (we) are vain and false within.[20]

In other words, what Shan-tao and Hōnen had taught as something to be avoided, i.e., falsehood within while making the appearance of piety, i.e., hypocrisy, Shinran declared to be the general condition of beings. He had stated that "(Beings) are defiled, evil and polluted, without a pure mind. They are false and vain and possess no mind of truth."[21]

Further Shinran's insight into his own evil nature altered decisively his orientation to, and treatment of, Pure Land doctrine. Influenced by his understanding of existence, he formulated a theory of religious process which at once indicates his relation to the tradition as an exponent of Pure Land thought and at the same time reveals his freedom from the tradition which enabled him to adapt it to his own religious experience.

In order to clarify his relation to the Pure Land tradition, Shinran formulated a theory of religious development which has come to be known as the process of turning through three Vows, the Nineteenth, Twentieth and Eighteenth, respectively. These Vows all pertain to the method of attaining birth into the Pure Land. Representing stages in spiritual development, the movement through each indicates the transition from self power to complete reliance on the Other Power. The presupposition behind the theory was Shinran's own experience of failure and frustration in Buddhist discipline and its transcendence through faith in Amida Buddha.

The description of the process in the *Kyōgyōshinshō*[22] is abstract and formal and employs the traditional terms of Pure Land teaching. Nevertheless the entire passage is suffused with his personal feeling and it represents his interpretation of the course of his own life.

The Nineteenth Vow[23] summarizes the ideal of Buddhism in which the devotee arouses a desire for enlightenment and engages in the practice of all

---

[18]*SSZ.,* I, 533.

[19]Coates and Ishizuka, *op. cit.,* II, 348.

[20]*SSZ.,* II, 652-653. *Kyōgyōshinshō,* Daiei Kaneko, (Annot.) (Tōkyō: Fuanami Bunko, 1958), 135.

[21]*Ibid.,* 152-153. Yamabe and Akanuma, *op. cit.,* II, 596-603.

[22]*Ibid.,* 165.

[23]See above p. 3.

forms of virtue. Thus aspiration and practice were regarded by Shinran as based in human resolution, and from his own experience on Mount Hiei he came to see that the ideal was doomed to failure because of the weakness of the human mind and the power of the passions.[24] Failing to meet the demand of this Vow, Shinran turned to the easy way represented by the Twentieth Vow. According to his interpretation, the practice of the "roots of merit" sanctioned by the Vow referred to the recitation of Amida Buddha's name which was the traditional practice of the Pure Land school. He was led to reject this ideal because he saw that it was also based on self-assertion.[25] The Twentieth Vow[26] was but a halfway point in the quest for salvation and is sometimes called the "half self-half Other Power" way. As Shinran's sense of sin and spiritual inability became more acute he realized that this position was basically inconsistent. The practice was given to those destitute of goodness, but yet required a measure of good in order to be effective.

The solution to his spiritual problem was discovered in faith founded on the Eighteenth Vow.[27] While we shall discuss his understanding of this Vow below, we may point out that the transition of this third stage signified the abandonment of all forms of egoistic self-assertion on the part of the devotee. Here Shinran eradicated any suggestion of self power from his concept of religion.

Not only is this theory novel in itself but its implications for the understanding of Pure Land thought by Shinran are also important. Previous teachers had accepted each Vow as given by Amida Buddha and therefore the basis for a variety of practices. Not until Hōnen, were other practices clearly ruled out as unsuitable for gaining salvation. While the general stream of Pure Land teaching accepted all Vows equally, and Hōnen simply singled out one, rejecting the rest, Shinran felt the need for a more consistent view. He did not accept them all equally, nor did he reject all in the interest of one. Rather he saw the Nineteenth and Twentieth Vows as having the function of leading an individual to faith in Amida Buddha according to the Eighteenth Vow through the gradual development of a sense of sin and failure in the devotee. This relation of the Vows may be compared to the relation of the Law and Gospel taught by the Apostle Paul in Romans 7 and Galatians 3. The Vows were merely instrumental to lead men to faith as the Law is the schoolmaster which points to the Gospel. In this way Shinran was able to retain a basis in the earlier tradition and at the same time to establish a basis for his own interpretations. He was also enabled to show a positive basis for the acceptance of the evil self in which the awareness of sin was but the first step to salvation. Most important, this theory enabled Shinran to avoid the pitfalls of earlier thought which, though proclaiming to be based in Other Power, actually cultivated salvation through self power.

[24] *Ibid.*, 154.
[25] *Ibid.*, 165.

[26] See above p. 3.
[27] See pp. 2-3.

In a similar manner to the way in which he adjusted the three Vows, Shinran also related the three major sutras of the tradition, again in such a fashion as to preserve his connection to the tradition, but also his freedom to interpret his insights into it. According to him the three sutras have a double relationship. There is the evident, surface one which emphasized the different religious tendencies of the texts. From this standpoint the *Kammuryōjukyō* represents the Nineteenth Vow, the *Amidakyō*, the Twentieth, and the *Muryōjukyō*, the Eighteenth. Such a relationship indicates that Shinran was clearly aware of the contradictory tendencies of Pure Land tradition. However, the second relation establishes the fundamental unity of the three texts by maintaining that they have one inner meaning which is the principle of faith taught in the *Muryōjukyō*. Here we can observe that he was not an arbitrary thinker who was willing to overthrow all traditional thought in favor of his own, but he was also moved by his own experience to seek ways in which that insight should not be compromised. In the effort to maintain a positive relation to the tradition Shinran introduced some novel views into his interpretation.

Another area in which we see the effect of Shinran's intense awareness of sin and evil is in his own critical classification of Buddhist doctrines which he developed to spell out precisely his relation to the general tradition. In order to indicate his idea we shall have to go back a bit and point out that Hōnen had also formed a critical classification based on the distinctions given in previous Pure Land teachers and designed to establish that the recitation of the name of Amida Buddha was the only true practice which would bring salvation. We have already noted that T'an-luan introduced the distinction self and Other Power into this thought. Tao-ch'o distinguished paths in Buddhism as Holy Path or Pure Land of which the Holy Path came to be regarded as self power and the Pure Land as based on Other Power. Shan-tao had designated within the Pure Land the five true practices as against the mixed practices of other ways. These five true practices were further analysed into the one true practice, recitation of the name of Amida Buddha, and the four auxiliary practices. Implicitly the way of recitation was superior, but the other practices also helped. Hōnen took over this basic outlook, but he stressed more strongly that the really assured way was the simple recitation of the name. True Pure Land teaching for Hōnen meant his own teaching as against the Pure Land teaching which was a subsidiary aspect of other school of contemporary Buddhism in his time.

Shinran followed Hōnen's interpretation in the definition of the relation of the practice of recitation to other Buddhist practices, but he probed deeper into the nature of that practice. He realized that not all vocal recitations were of the same character, and he proposed the distinction between True and Provisional Pure Land teaching. The provisional teaching employed the way of recitation as Hōnen had taught, but the attitude of the devotee was marked by self-assertion. Through this practice the individual regards himself as acquiring merit, cultivating virtue, or achieving his own salvation. Against this standpoint Shinran declared the True Pure Land teaching in which one must rely entirely upon the Vow of Amida Buddha without a moment's doubt. He claimed there was no act by which salvation could be attained, and he regarded salvation as entirely a gift, the result of Amida Buddha's transfer of merit to save all beings which we shall discuss below in more detail.

Through his doctrinal classification, Shinran attempted to indicate that salvation is by faith alone, and nothing more is required of the believer than an awareness of his sin, a strong faith and a sense of gratitude to the Buddha. We must now move on to discuss the nature of faith in Shinran's thought.

IV

FAITH:

ITS DEFINITION

As we have already indicated, it is the outstanding feature of Shinran's thought that he made faith the primary or root cause for the achievement of salvation. He was led to this insight by his own religious experience and his understanding that mortal existence is completely depraved. In view of the fact that men have no foundation within their own capacity for achieving salvation on their own, he had to probe deeply into the nature of Amida Buddha and his Vows. The key to this way he discovered in simple faith.

Since Amida Buddha had achieved salvation for evil mortals, Shinran throughout his writings exhorted men to place their faith in him and thereby to give up their anxious concern for their future destiny. He found considerable support for his exaltation of faith in the Buddhist tradition, and he appropriated these passages for his own view,[1] though, as we shall see, he interpreted faith in a distinctively new way.

Shinran frequently wrote to his disciples and urged them to maintain their faith in Amida Buddha, and not allow themselves to be diverted into attempts to secure salvation through their own power.

> If you believe that it is the mystery of Buddha wisdom, you should not strive for this and that and be particularly confused. You should not even have doubts when people say this and that. Only entrust yourself to the profound Vow of the Tathagata (Amida Buddha).[2]

He recognized the paradoxical character of faith in that the way of faith established by Amida Buddha is called the easy path in Buddhism. Yet it is perhaps the most difficult path to undertake because men are always tempted to strive for their own salvation rather than simply relying on the Buddha.[3] Egotism, pride or despair may bar a man from faith.

---

[1] *Ibid.*, 64 furnishes an eloquent example from the *Kegonkyō*.

[2] *Ibid.*, 671.

[3] *Ibid.*, 48, 165-166.

There are several aspects to Shinran's understanding of faith which will engage our attention here. From the standpoint of Amida Buddha or looking from what may be called the divine side of faith, we see that he described the nature of faith according to three aspects presented in the Eighteenth Vow. Further, he also identified the essence of faith with the traditional concept of Buddha nature. In both of these points we can observe significant reinterpretations. From the standpoint of the human individual, he viewed faith as the absence of doubt in Amida Buddha's Vows, and as we shall see below in the discussion of the process of the arising of faith, and also in the interpretation of religious devotion, faith was identified with the practice of recitation of the name. Also our discussion below relating to the acceptance by Amida Buddha's light in the process of the arising of faith will show that an important aspect of the religious consciousness which he called faith was the awareness in the individual of his passion-ridden nature and need of Amida Buddha's compassion. His conception of faith therefore was a very comprehensive understanding embracing the meaning of faith in terms of divine reality, and as it was experienced in the finite individual.

We would call attention here to the fact which we shall develop later that the most significant feature of Shinran's interpretation of faith is that he regarded it totally as a gift of Amida Buddha, and this understanding supplied the theological basis for the other aspects of his interpretation of religion.

When Shinran attempted to discover a description of faith which would not convey the connotation of a faith generated by human resolution of will, he was attracted to the three spiritual attitudes given in the Eighteenth Vow. Pure Land teachers had discussed faith in terms of the three mental attitudes of the *Kammuryōjukyō,* and they had also viewed the Eighteenth Vow primarily from the standpoint of the discipline which could be interpreted in the phrase "till ten thoughts." As he clearly observed these two aspects of Pure Land doctrine pointed to a self power ideal in which men strive to gain salvation for themselves.

The three elements which Shinran distinguished in the Eighteenth Vow were the Sincere Mind, Trustfulness, and a Desire for rebirth (into the Pure Land). It will be noted that these terms do not appear to differ significantly from the three mental attitudes of the *Kammuryōjukyō* such as Sincerity, Deep Mind and Desire for rebirth through transfer of merit. The distinction between Shinran and the traditional view at this point is the theological context and what is implied by it. Shinran focused his attention in the Eighteenth Vow on these spiritual attitudes rather than the discipline aspect emphasized by previous teachers. He implied by this that as Amida Buddha had given the discipline by which men could be saved, he also gave the mind which precedes and moves the individual to take up the discipline.

While these three spiritual attitudes are seen by Shinran as the gift of Amida Buddha, as we shall discuss later, the Sincere Mind, or the mind of truth, is regarded as the seed from which the other two aspects emerge. That is, the chief feature of Amida Buddha's endeavor to achieve salvation for beings lies in his utter sincerity and truthfulness from which he never deviated for even a single second in the long course of his work. His mind is characterized by the deep sincerity of his compassionate intention. It is this mind or attitude which, when given to man mysteriously, arouses his trust and desire to be born into the Pure Land. Shinran gave a deeper theological foundation to the understanding of the nature of faith in viewing it as a reflection of the very spirit of Amida Buddha himself, as well as showing that it was not a contrivance of man but a fruit of the Buddha's aspiration.

The second important interpretation of faith which Shinran made was his assertion that faith within men is the achievement of Buddha nature. This interpretation is related to the previous point in that the Buddha nature is synonymous with the Buddha mind and essentially refers to the same phenomenon given immediately above.

Despite the essential identity of the content of the concepts as they were taken up by Shinran, the assertion that faith is Buddha nature is important for seeing his creative reinterpretation of traditional doctrine. In this belief he appropriated one of the most fundamental doctrines of Mahayana Buddhism which Pure Land teachers had tended to overlook in their emphasis on the degenerate nature of mortal existence. However, his experience of the deep sinfulness of mortal nature gave him deeper insight into the nature of Other Power than earlier Pure Land thinkers. As the nature of Amida Buddha was conceived in absolute terms, he was able to revive this concept of the universal Buddha nature as a support for Other Power faith.

The concept of Buddha nature in all beings for Shinran was no longer a foundation for a theory and process of purifying practices and meditations intended to manifest the latent Buddha nature within man. Instead of a process of self realization where one comes to see his nature as Buddha, one becomes more aware of his sinful nature and his need of the Buddha's power to gain release.

Within Shinran's interpretation there are two aspects that are coordinated. On the one hand, he saw a great gulf between mortal life and the Buddha which was impossible to span from the side of beings. On the other hand, the fundamental unity that he saw between mortals and the Buddha, which was also held to exist in Mahayana thought, Shinran claimed came completely from the side of the Buddha through the gift of faith as the transfer of his qualities of mind. In other words, it was by the Buddha's act of compassion that one attains Buddha nature.[4] Shinran based his interpretation on the *Nehangyō* which was the source of the concept of Buddha nature in Mahayana Buddhism:

---

[4]Shinryū Umehara, *Kyogyōshinshō Shinshaku* (Toyama-ken: Senchōji Bunsho Dendōbu, 1957), II, 229-237. Yamabe and Akanuma, *op. cit.*, II, 717-724. Taneuchi, *op. cit.*, 226-227.

> The Nirvana sutra states' "O good men! We call the great mercy and the great pity 'Buddha nature.' Why? (Because) the great mercy and the great pity follow the Bodhisattva as a shadow follows form. All beings assuredly are able to attain the great mercy and great pity ultimately. Therefore we say that all beings have the Buddha nature. Great mercy and great pity are called Buddha nature... Buddha nature is called the great faith... All beings assuredly attain great faith ultimately. Therefore it is taught that all beings have Buddha nature. Great faith is itself Buddha nature ...[5]

This passage was interpreted by Shinran in line with his understanding that all spiritual benefit proceeds *from* the Buddha to beings. For him the Buddha nature was not a metaphysical concept intended to show that mortals were all essentially Buddhas and grounded in the same reality. Though Shinran may have believed that there was a common metaphysical bond which linked beings and Buddha, he did not employ this idea to establish a system of practice to realize essential Buddha nature. Thus he wrote:

> Tathagata is Nirvana'
> Nirvana is called Buddha nature.
> Unable to realize enlightenment in the land of mortals,
> We will attain in the Land of Bliss.[6]

Shinran took a completely religious view of this concept and defined the attainment of Buddha nature in this life as the existence of faith within man as the result of Buddha's activity:

> One who lives in faith is equal
> To Tathagata, the Buddha.
> Great Faith is the Buddha Nature'
> This at once is Tathagata.[7]

Shinran perceived correctly in the passage from the *Nehangyō* that Buddha nature meant the qualities of the Buddha that operate to bring beings to enlightenment, i.e., his compassion. Buddha nature therefore refers essentially to the Tathagata's work of salvation, and this is realized in the faith which is aroused in men. Taken in this light, the text becomes a support for the theory of absolute Other Power in which salvation derives fully from the Buddha, and is experienced as faith within man.

The third concept of faith which is outstanding in Shinran's interpretation is his idea that the three spiritual attitudes which we have discussed above are united within the experience of the individual as the absence of doubt in Amida Buddha's work of salvation. The doubt to which Shinran referred was not merely intellectual doubt resulting from uncertainties of knowledge, but

[5] *SSZ.*, II, 62-63.
[6] *Ibid.*, 497.   [7] *Ibid.*

it may be called religious doubt in which the individual, refusing to rely on the Buddha's power to gain salvation, strives on his own. Doubt is synonymous with the self power attitude and he regarded it as a most serious sin which calls for deep repentance.[8]

In order to show that the absence of doubt is the essence of faith, Shinran analysed the three attitudes given in the Eighteenth Vow such as Sincere mind, Trustfulness, and Desire for Birth. According to his analysis, the element that establishes the unity of these three aspects of faith as they take form in man is that in each case there is not a speck of doubt. This analysis is concisely summarized in the *Kyōgyōshinshō:*

> We clearly know that "Shishin" is itself the mind which has the seed of true sincerity. Therefore, doubts are never mixed in. "Shingyō" is itself the mind filled with true sincerity... "Yokushō" is the mind that knows and realizes the joy of the Vow... Therefore, doubt never mixes in... Truly we know that since doubt does not interfere, it is called faith.[9]

Behind Shinran's insistence on the seriousness of doubt lay concern for two types of individuals. He tried to appeal to the individual who did not believe that he was good enough to be saved, and to the individual who had confidence in his own good deeds.

Those who believed they were too sinful to be saved by Amida Buddha had already been encountered by Hōnen. Like Hōnen, Shinran had repeatedly to console such individuals with the assurance that Amida Buddha made evil persons the specific object of his salvation.[10] Encouraging evil men to faith, he reminded them that "as His Vow is thus specifically meant for them, they need not feel humiliated because of their evil karma."[11]

The second type of individual about whom Shinran was concerned was the person who believed that he was able in himself, apart from Amida Buddha's work, to gain salvation for himself. With such people in mind, he declared that faith was difficult to attain, despite the fact that it is termed the "easy path." Thus he commented:

> For evil men with pride and false views
> Faith in the Nembutsu of Amida Buddha's Original Vow
> Is extremely hard to accept.
> Nothing exceeds this most difficult among the difficult.[12]

Self confidence and self righteousness in religion were considered by Shinran as the grand illusion. In contrast with the absolute purity and compassion

[8]*Ibid.;* 525.

[9]*Ibid.,* 59. See also 68.

[10]*Ibid.,* 777-778.

[11]Suzuki, *Miscellany on the Shin Teaching of Buddhism, op. cit.,* 143.

[12]*SSZ.,* II, 44, 454. Umehara, *op. cit.,* II, 34-36.

of Amida Buddha no good deeds are possible for mortal beings. Driven by inescapable passions, beings cannot avoid the essential egoism that infects all mortal action. He concurred with Shan-tao who long before had declared that "(These people) never think to repay the grace of that Buddha. Even when they do deeds and practices, in their minds they give rise to arrogance and pride. They always seek fame. Enveloped in their own egos, they do not approach intimately their compassions and good teachers . . ."[13]

Both types of individuals, the sinner and the good man, were in a desperate situation because their understanding of Buddhism prevented them from availing themselves of the salvation offered by Amida Buddha. Each suffered from the same basic misunderstanding of Buddhism. They interpreted Buddhism legalistically and viewed the way of salvation as merely a matter of following the rules and acquiring sufficient merit to gain Nirvana. With this attitude, true faith, though the easy way to salvation, was the most difficult to accept.[14]

The evil man, in view of such an understanding of religion, was doomed out of hand. He simply could not measure up, and knowing it, he probably gave up in despair. The legalistic view crushed his hope and left him with an unresolved anxiety as to his future destiny. Shinran was very sympathetic to such people, for he acknowledged also that he carried a burden of sin.

The good man, confident in his goodness, might become hypocritical or calculating as he strives to gain salvation. Religion for such persons may become a form of self serving and a source of pride. Shinran regarded pride in one's goodness as reprehensible, and he maintained that belief in one's goodness was a barrier to attainment of enlightenment.

Shinran's faith in Amida Buddha's Vows was so great that he declared there was no evil which could obstruct its work, and there was no good superior to it. Thus he maintained that the evil man need not fear for his salvation, because Amida Buddha has already accomplished it, and the good man should give up his petty good deeds which cannot surpass the goodness of Amida Buddha.[15] All men good or evil should give themselves up in faith which transcends any form of legalistic demand.[16]

Although Shinran understood that faith is a gift of Amida Buddha, he realized that this faith only came to fruition or consciousness when individuals turned away from their self power attempts to gain salvation and placed their reliance solely in him. Thus throughout his writings we find many exhortations in which he urges men to firm and deep faith in Amida Buddha.[17] He realized it was necessary to call men continually to faith else they would ever follow their inclinations to strive for salvation themselves. He insisted that men give up all

---

[13] *Ibid.*, 166.
[14] *Ibid.*, 165, 48.
[15] *Ibid.*, 773, 786.
[16] *Ibid.*, 775.
[17] *Ibid.*, 486, 671, 786.

forms of self-assertion. The rejection of all human forms of contriving gave a distinctive character to the religious life for it no longer meant the separation of the individual from the ordinary demands of life.

His exaltation of faith as the only way of salvation opened the door to a new understanding of existence as he taught men to accept themselves for what they are, passion-ridden mortals lacking any capacity to free themselves from its bondage. In view of self-acceptance, all legalistic, meritorious practices were rejected and with them such traditional ways of Buddhism as monasticism, celibacy and abstention from eating meat or intoxicating beverages. There was no asceticism or religious privation and no need to appease Buddhas or gods in order to win their acceptance or assistance in gaining some goal. Only trust in Amida Buddha who accepts the most sinful as well as the most righteous was required.

This new way of life which grew out of Shinran's thought has sometimes been termed "naturalism." The Japanese term for it is Kono Mama, and perhaps the words of the Christian hymn, "Just as I am" depict the sentiment behind the term. Because one is accepted as he is by the compassionate Buddha, one can take life just as it is, as one finds it, and in the midst of this life find the ultimate reality. It is clear that this understanding of existence owes much to the influence of Taoism as it was transmitted into Buddhism. Shinran was able to adapt this thought to the Pure Land teaching of salvation through Amida Buddha. He went beyond the tradition in providing a solid metaphysical and religious understanding for the life of faith.

He set forth his understanding in a famous passage called the *Jinenhōnishō*[18] which he wrote in his eighty-sixth year. It has been regarded as the highest point of his philosophical and religious interpretation of existence. Though the statement was brief, it stressed those points which are the foundation of life within the perspective of faith in Amida Buddha. Here he interpreted the term Jinen Hōni, which means "absolute truth" and corresponds to the Taoist idea of Tao, in a way to indicate that salvation is completely dependent on the work of Amida Buddha:

> When we speak of "Nature" (Jinen), the character Ji (自) means naturally, by itself (Onozukara). It is not (the result of) an intention (self-assertion-Hakarai) of the devotee. Nen (然) is a word which means "to cause to come about" (Shikarashimu). Shikarashimu (also signifies that it) is not (due to any) effort (Hakarai) of the devotee. Since it is (the result of) the Vow of the Tathagata, we call it Hōni (法爾), i.e., truth. We say of Hōni that it "causes to come about," because it is the Vow of the Tathagata. Since the truth is the Vow of the Tathagata, we say generally that it is not (the result) of the effort of the devotee, and therefore the power (virtue) of this Dharma is that it "causes to be." For the first time, there is nothing to be done by man. This is what we should understand as "the reason which is beyond reason" (Mugi no Gi). Originally Jinen was a word meaning

---

[18]See Tomitarō Karasawa, *Shinran no Sekai* (Tōkyō: Kobundo, 1953), 46-56, for a discussion of this passage.

"to cause to be." We say Jinen when the devotee does not consider his goodness or evil in accordance with the fact that Amida has vowed originally (that salvation was to be attained) not by the efforts of the devotee, but by being embraced and caused to rely on the Namu Amida Butsu (his name). In the Vow which we hear, it is vowed that he will cause us (to attain) the highest Buddhahood. "Highest Buddhahood" signifies to abide in formlessness. Because we are without form, we say Jinen (nature). When we indicate that there is form, we do not speak of the highest Nirvana. We have heard and learned for the first time that the one who makes known formlessness is called Amida. Amida is the means by which we are caused to know formlessness. After we understand this principle we should not constantly discuss Jinen (nature). If we constantly discuss it, the principle that "what is beyond reason is reason" is made (to conform to) reason. This is the mystery of the Buddha-wisdom.[19]

According to this text the primary characteristic of the life of faith for Shinran is the negation of self-assertion. The rejection of self-assertion is based on the fact that everything "is caused to be;" things are as they are. Behind the terminology of this passage we can see the Buddhist rendition of the Taoist understanding of nature as the indefinable, formless reality which is the ground of discriminated, finite beings. Its mode of operation as the pattern for the religious life rather than its metaphysical character was uppermost in the thought of the Taoists and the Buddhists who took over the idea. Here emphasis was placed on the apparent effortless activity of nature in which nothing is done, but everything happens. Spontaneity, unconscious and uncontrived activity are traits of the way of nature and the mode of existence.

In making the activity of Amida Buddha's Vows correlative with the working of nature, Shinran gave a deep philosophical foundation to his view of faith in which the devotee's identification with Amida Buddha symbolizes the identification of the devotee and nature. Thus to do what is natural, what is uncontrived, and spontaneous has the highest religious significance. Further, Shinran maintains in the passage that this identification means that even the lowest devotee attains the highest spiritual goal, the bliss of Nirvana. The emphasis on the idea of "causing to be" brings us to the question of the arising of faith in Shinran's teaching.

---

[19]*SSZ.*, II, 663-664.

V

FAITH: ITS ARISING

Faith as a gift of Amida Buddha.—We now come to a discussion of one of Shinran's most significant insights which certainly qualifies him for a place among the great religious thinkers of the world, and clearly comparable to the Protestant Reformers, Luther and Calvin, in whose thought faith as the gift of God's grace worked a revolution in Christian theology. It should be pointed out here that the understanding of faith as a gift of the deity and determined by that deity does not inhibit preaching for conversion or the necessity of decision to accept the way of salvation. In this Shinran stands on common ground with thinkers in Christianity and Islam. For though Amida Buddha is the source of faith, Shinran continues to preach. In religious thought of this type, it is believed that the proclamation of the message affords the opportunity for salvation to be realized by the individual. The point at which conversion is achieved is considered the time when the deity grants salvation. Thus we find also an idea of conversion in Shinran which is the decisive moment for the individual.

This insight into faith on the part of Shinran extends its influence to every doctrine which he taught. Already in our discussion we have seen that the point at which Shinran departed from traditional thought was determined by his desire to emphasize the fact that faith, or salvation, is not due at all to the contriving action of man, but solely through the power of Amida Buddha. He reconciled the apparent contradiction between the theological interpretation of faith as the work of Amida Buddha and the human experience in which a man actually appears to make the decisive act of faith. He did this by indicating that what one is aware of as his act of faith or believing is actually the manifestation of Amida Buddha's gift of faith in his mind.[1]

The principle that faith is a gift of Amida Buddha is set forth in the volume on faith in the *Kyōgyōshinshō* where Shinran takes up in detail the essential nature of faith. In the course of his writing, he gives a very concise statement of the theory:

---

[1]*Ibid.*, 48 for a paradoxical statement of these two aspects of faith.

The mind of the Buddha is difficult to understand, but if we may infer concerning his mind. (we might say) that the whole sea of sentient beings, from the beginning-less past even until the present time, are defiled, impure and stained. Their minds are not pure, and being false, they do not have a mind of truth. For this reason, the Tathagata had compassion on the whole sea of suffering sentient beings. For incomprehensibly infinite kalpas he performed the disciplines of a Bodhisattva, and never for even a single moment were his practices of the mouth, mind or body, impure, or untrue. By his pure, sincere mind, the Tathagata perfected his com-pletely harmonious, unimpeded, mysterious, inexpressible, incomprehensible, supreme virtue. *He transferred the sincere mind of the Tathagata to all the sea of sentient beings who are passionridden, evil in deed and in mind.* Hence this manifests the true mind for helping others therefore it was never mixed with doubts. Hence this sincere mind has his virtuous name as its essence.[2]

However, in order to clarify more adequately the importance of this insight we must first briefly indicate the nature of faith in the general Buddhist tradi-tion. It is evident in this tradition that faith is regarded as an act of the will, aroused by the individual and directed toward the Buddha, his teaching and his community of followers. Thus a leading Western expositor of Buddhism describes the act of faith in Buddhism:

In Theravada Buddhism faith is the faith of a traveller in a famous guide. The Guide has pointed the way which he has trodden and the traveller, nothing doubt-ing, follows in that Way.[3]

A modern Theravada Buddhist also expresses a similar understanding:

A man first learns about the Buddha's teaching by hearsay. Then he tests what he has heard as far as he can. When he has done this enough to feel convinced that it is reliable, he outwardly expresses his conviction by pronouncing the three Refuges, the *Saranattaya* or *Tissarana* as they are called in Pali. And afterwards, whenever he has the occasion outwardly to reaffirm that inner conviction, he does so by pronouncing them aloud.[4]

Recently a Japanese Buddhist in a discussion of faith in Buddhism and Chris-tianity, has defined the faith of a Buddhist in terms of a strong resolve:

Faith through understanding is to listen to a teaching, understand it, and then come to a decision that there is no other teaching than this on which one can depend. Thereupon he becomes converted, and fervently tries to follow the teach-ing. He no longer looks to right and left, but turns to one direction, singleminded. This state of mind is faith. A sutra says: *"Bodhisattva* (Buddha-to-be), at his first conversion, earnestly seeks bodhi (wisdom) and is too firm to be moved."* This is the faith through understanding. His faith is firm and intense, based on under-standing and conviction.[5]

[2]Yamabe and Akanuma, *op. cit.,* I, 87-89 gives a detailed discussion of Ekō, Shinran's reinterpretation and his textual supports.

[3]Humphreys, *Buddhism, op. cit.,* 61.

[4]Bhikku Nanamoli, *The Three Refuges,* tract, *Bodhi Leaves,* #5, (Buddhist Publication Society: Kandy, Ceylon), 1.

[5]Fumio Masutani, *A Comparative Study of Buddhism and Christianity* (Tōkyō: Young East Assoc., 1957), 68-79.

In the declaration of refuge in the three treasures, the traditional mark of Buddhism: "I take refuge in the Buddha; I take refuge in the Dharma, I take refuge in the Sangha," the devotee reveals his resolve to place all reliance on the Buddha and his teaching as the way to liberation. There is no question that faith has always been an essential element in the Buddhist religious life, but it has generally been a faith which is the result of inquiry and decision cultivated by the devotee himself.

Faith has always played a particularly conspicuous role in the aspiration for birth in the Pure Land. Faith was always considered a necessary prerequisite to the discipline and practices which would bring that birth. Nagarjuna, who was considered by Shinran as the first patriarch in the Pure Land tradition, wrote:

> If good men and women hear that Buddha's name and obtain deep faith, then they do not regress from (the state of) anuttara samyaksambodhi.[6]

Nagarjuna also distinguished the "easy practice of the means of faith (Shinhō-benigyō)"[7] from the difficult practices in Buddhism. Vasubandhu also called men and women to arouse faith and practice the five gates of devotion.[8] For himself Vasubandhu declared:

> O World-honored One, I, singleheartedly, take refuge in the Tathagata of Universal, unimpeded Light, and desire to be born in His Land of Bliss.[9]

The character of faith was discussed in T'an-luan's commentary to Vasubandhu's treatise on the Pure Land. T'an-luan declared that the content of faith was singlehearted refuge (reliance, faith) in Amida Buddha and desire for birth in this Pure Land.[10] This singlehearted faith was to be manifested in continuous and uninterrupted thought on the Buddha and his land.

When T'an-luan discussed the hindrances to true practice, he explained that they were the lack of ardent faith, the lack of deep faith and the lack of continuity (steadfastness). These factors were all interrelated so that the lack of any element meant the lack of all. The presence or absence of these aspects of faith determined the condition of the devotee's singlehearted faith.[11]

T'an-luan placed the greatest stress in his understanding of faith on the aspect of continuity. He pointed out that the continuous repetition of the name of the Buddha would cleanse the devotee of eighty millions of kalpas of sins as the *Kammuryōjukyō* taught.[12] In his discussion of the number of recitations that were needed to assure birth in the Pure Land, he held that the important thing was that the recitation, or thought of the Buddha, be continuous and one need not be concerned greatly with the exact number itself.[13]

[6] *SSZ.*, I, 255.　　[9] *Ibid.*, 269.　　[12] *Ibid.*, 282.

[7] *Ibid.*, 254.　　[10] *Ibid.*, 282.　　[13] *Ibid.*, 311.

[8] *Ibid.*, 270.　　[11] *Ibid.*, 314.

We can observe in T'an-luan's conception of faith that he stood deep within a meditative tradition. In this tradition the condition of the mind in approaching meditation was all-important in achieving the goal of meditation. In the meditative approach, purification of the mind and steadfastness (singleheartedness) were essential in the realization of the goal of insight and enlightenment. Purification preceded insight; concentration and unification of the mind preceded contemplation. In the traditional system of discipline it was no problem to justify the necessity for the purification of the mind as a preliminary step in the path of meditation. A problem arose in the Pure Land tradition as to how mediocre, evil mortals who commit the five deadly sins and ten evil acts could attain the required purification or steadfastness of mind. T'an-luan did not clarify the dilemma, but he was outstanding in calling attention to the nature of the faith needed to gain rebirth in the Pure Land through the practice of recitation. After him the concept of single-hearted faith became an important focal point of Pure Land doctrine.[14]

Shan-tao, as we have seen previously, also analysed in detail the mind of faith required for birth in the Pure Land. In his commentary on the *Kammuryōjukyō*, he taught that the practice of recitation was to be performed with a sincere mind, deep faith and strong desire for birth. According to him sincerity must pervade all practices. One must believe deeply that he is a sinner chained to the wheel of transmigration, as well as believing deeply that he can be saved by Amida Buddha's Vows. All the devotee's merits in practices are to be directed toward birth in the Pure Land.

It is clear from our survey of Buddhist tradition that faith is conceived as an operation of the human will in which the individual in full sincerity turns his aspirations and his efforts toward the attainment of Buddhist ideals.

Shinran's personal religious experience caused him to diverge widely from the Buddhist tradition. So compelling was his insight that he had to rend the grammar of the sutra in order to get an authoritative, textual basis for it.

Shinran read his epoch-making insight into the text of the *Muryojukyo* where it relates the fulfillment of the Eighteenth Vow by Amida Buddha. He was enabled to do this through the application of certain Japanese principles of grammar devised for reading Chinese texts. When he applied the Japanese grammar to the Chinese text, he implied that faith and the thought of Amida Buddha were transferred to beings by the Buddha himself. According to the Chinese text read strictly, the sutra reads:

> If all those beings hear that name, believe and rejoice even for one thought (moment), and sincerely transfer (the merit of the thought) desiring to be born in that Land, then they will obtain rebirth and abide in the state of non-retrogression. Only those are excluded who have committed the five deadly sins and

[14]Keishin Nagata, "The Commentary on Singleness of Heart in the Ronchu," *Indogaku Bukkyōgaku Kenkyū* III-2 (6) (March 1955), 532-533.

slandered the Dharma.[15]

However, Shinran read the text according to his insight in the following manner:

> If all beings who hear that name, believe and rejoice, even for one moment, as a result of the fact that (Amida) has sincerely transferred (His Name), and desire to be born in that country, they will obtain birth and abide in the state of non-retrogression, excluding those alone who have committed the five deadly sins and slandered the Dharma.[16]

The problem in the alteration of the grammar of this text revolves about the term Shishin Ekō. Shishin Ekō normally means to "transfer with a true or sincere mind." In traditional Buddhism, transfers of merit are usually made by a devotee toward some spiritual object or benefit which one desires. When the practice of recitation is viewed as a means to salvation, the salvation comes about when the merit acquired through the recitation is directed toward the goal of birth in the Pure Land.

In Shinran's thought the perspective is entirely reversed. *All transfer of merit comes from Amida Buddha to man.* From our discussion of the degenerate nature of beings in his thought, it is clear that beings have nothing to transfer since they are deeply evil. Yet Amida Buddha as the absolute source of salvation has the merit to give to beings to bring about their salvation. Thus Shinran's insight overpowered the normal grammatical interpretation of the text.[17] This can be evidenced from the fact that the verbal ending Seshimetamaeri is put into the mouth of the Buddha. As an honorific form, one would not use it of himself or of persons below himself. Shinran, however, desired to point out clearly that all spiritual benefit proceeded from Amida Buddha. He alone is the source of virtue and merit. Further the grammatical relation of the phrase Shishin ni Ekō Seshimetamaeri and the phrases preceding and following are not clear. The disruption of the thought of the Chinese is due to Shinran's insight and his desire to stress the fact that Amida Buddha is the ultimate ground of salvation. This interpretation is further clarified in the

---

[15] *SSZ.*, I, 24.

[16] *Ibid.*

[17] Another interesting example of Shinran's subjectivity in the treatment of traditional texts can be found in the way in which he employed Shan-tao's description of Amida Buddha's sincerity in his volume on faith in the *Kyōgyō-shinshō* and in the volume on the transformed land. In the volume on faith, Shinran quoted the part of the passage giving the three minds as outlined by Shan-tao. It is significant, however, that Shinran deleted a passage dealing with ethical and religious exhortation. The material which was deleted in the faith volume was later used in the volume on the transformed land to typify the ideal of the devotees of self power.

The question is raised why did Shinran cut up the passage in this way? The answer lies in his endeavor to show in the faith volume that the three winds, (sincerity, deep mind and the mind of transfer and aspiration) were given as gifts to men from Amida Buddha, as a result of his aspiration to save all beings. Any text which could be made to imply this transfer on the part of Amida Buddha was appropriated by Shinran for the faith volume. In the case of the initially deleted portion which was used in the volume on the transformed land, the grammar and content were such that it clearly referred to beings and not to the activity of the Buddha. Therefore, it could not be used in the faith volume.

Ichinentannenmoni where Shinran gives a word interpretation of the passage in question;

> The term Shoushūjō signifies all the beings in the universe. Mongomyōgō (hearing that name) is to hear the name of the Original Vow (i.e. the name of Amida). "To hear" means to hear of the Original Vow and not to have a doubting mind. Further "to hear" is the principle that manifests (the meaning of) faith. (In the phrase) Shinjinkangi naishi ichinen, Shinjin (faith) is to hear of the Vow of the Tathagata without any mind of doubt; Kan (joy) means to cause to rejoice with the body; Ki (joy) is to cause to rejoice in the mind. Previously the mind of rejoicing meant "not obtaining (now) what one will obtain (in the future)." Naishi signifies both many or few, far or near, before or after. It is an inclusive term. (The term) Ichinen reveals the smallest fraction of time when faith is obtained. In the phrase Shishin Ekō, Shishin is the word for truth (Shinjitsu). Truth is the mind of Amida Nyorai. Ekō is the principle in which (Amida) has given his name of the Original Vow to all the beings of the Universe.[18]

Shinryū Umehara points to several other passages which indicate Shinran's view of absolute Other Power, or the fact that Amida Buddha bestows ultimate salvation on man.[19] Shinran's treatment of the Chinese character reveals his insight into Other Power. In a passage from the *Muryōjukyō*[20] which Shinran interpreted in the *Songōshinzōmeimon*,[21] he wrote that beings who heard of the Vow Power and Amida Buddha's name, and desire to be born into the Pure Land, "naturally" attain the unretrogressive state. The term Ji (自) was interpreted as "naturally" and meant that the individual attained without any striving or calculating on his part. Rather the individual *is caused* to arrive there through the operation of nature which is the working of Amida Buddha and symbolized by his Vow.

Similarly Shinran saw the principle of absolute Other Power in the (横) Ō which appeared in the *Muryōjukyō*.[22] In the *Songōshinzōmeimon*,[23] this term has the sense of "crosswise," "transverse." In its use in such terms as Ōshi (横死), "violent death," Ōryō (横領), "seizing," and Ōbō (横暴), "oppression," there is implied the sense of suddenness. This sense of suddenness pointed to the instantaneous aspect of salvation for Shinran, and he saw

---

These examples of the arbitrary dividing of passages indicates that Shinran imposed his insight on the text and employed the text as subordinate to the insight. Throughout he shows great freedom in the handling of traditional texts. See *SSZ.*, II, 52 and 149; compare with I, 533-534. Also Yamabe and Akanuma, *op. cit.*, II, 607-608.

[18] *SSZ.*, II, 604-605. For discussion of this point the reader may be referred to Suzuki, *Miscellany on the Shin Teaching of Buddhism, op. cit.*, 23; 61-63. Also Umehara, *op. cit.*, II, 46-50. Karasawa, *Shinran no Sekai, op. cit.*, 138-141, shows that Shinran read this insight into passages which he quoted also from T'an-luan and Vasubandhu. Wherever the term Ekō appears, he interpreted it to refer only to the activity of Amida Buddha. Yamabe and Akanuma, *op. cit.*, I, 87-89 give a detailed discussion of Ekō, Shinran's reinterpretation and his textual supports.

[19] Shinryū Umehara, *Shinran Kyōgaku* (Toyamaken; Senchōji Bunsho Dendōbu, 1952), 66-79.

[20] *SSZ.*, I, 26.

[21] *Ibid.*, II, 579.

[22] *Ibid.*, I, 31.

[23] *Ibid.*, II, 580.

in it the operation of Buddha's Vow apart from the individual's striving or contrivance. Thus he wrote:

> Ō (橫) means "crosswise." "Crosswise" means that *it is not the contrivance of the devotee* because he believes in the Vow Power of the Tathagata. The five evil paths are "naturally" cut off and one is liberated from the four (types of) births. This we call "Crosswise," "Other Power." This is "Crosswise Transcendence" (橫超 Ōchō).[24]

Shinran also found similar significance in the term Soku, Sunawachi (即) which also appeared in the *Muryōjukyō*,[25] and was interpreted in the *Ichinentannenmoni*.[26] Here, he saw the word having the sense of principle, law or rule. It also had the meaning "thereupon" or "accordingly," and conveyed the idea that the succeeding statement followed the previous as its "natural," inevitable outcome. All contrivance or calculation on the part of the individual was again set aside. Thus he wrote:

> Soku (即) means Sunawachi (thereupon) or Nori (rule). When one believes in the Original Vow of the Tathagata for one moment, he is assuredly *caused to receive* unsurpassed virtue without soliciting it. Unconsciously he receives profound blessing. It is the law which manifests therefore various insights (Satori) naturally (Jinen).[27]

It is clear that the central point of Shinran's teaching concerning faith is not only that he made faith the primary cause for salvation, but that he insisted that *faith is not the result of human resolution to believe* or the cultivation individually of a sense of dependence. Other Pure Land teachers, and Buddhists through all periods had talked of the faith that was required for embarking on the discipline that would lead to release from the stream of birth and death. There is, however, a qualitative difference between Shinran's understanding of faith and that found in the Buddhist tradition before him. Shinran maintained that faith was aroused through the operation of Amida Buddha in the heart and mind of the individual, and this faith was the true cause of salvation. It was precisely because Amida Buddha gave the faith that faith, and faith alone, could be the true and only cause for birth in the Pure Land for defiled beings. From this significant change in the understanding of faith flow the important contributions of Shinran's thought.

Factors in the Appearance of Faith. — The belief that faith is a gift from Amida Buddha raises the question about the process by which faith becomes manifest in beings. We are not concerned here with the psychological characteristics of the appearance of faith, but with the theoretical understanding of its

---

[24] *Ibid.*

[25] *Ibid.*, I, 46. "Therefore, these are endowed with the highest virtue."

[26] *Ibid.*, II, 611.

[27] *Ibid.*

origin. The description of the actual arising of faith within man does not greatly differ in Shinran's thought from the traditional view, except in the qualification that what appears to us as "our" faith and sincerity is really the result of Amida Buddha's work in our minds. Shinran, therefore, can employ traditional descriptions of faith when depicting the nature of faith in man. It is his philosophical understanding of the origin of faith and its implications for religious existence that distinguishes his thought so sharply from previous Pure Land thinkers.

These are several aspects to Shinran's view of the process of the arising of faith in sentient beings. In the first place our attention is drawn to the significant interpretation which he placed on the Seventeenth Vow of Amida Buddha.[28] Secondly, we must discuss the operation of the name of Amida Buddha and his Light as the cause and condition for the appearance of faith in beings.

In order for Shinran to establish his insight into the absolute Other Power faith firmly, it was necessary for him to discover materials in the sutras and commentaries which he could use as evidence. The realization that faith was a gift from Amida Buddha and beyond human achievement naturally prompted the question: How does this faith arise? In his answer to the question, he made the Seventeenth Vow a central point in his explanation. In this Vow he discovered the universal basis for the origin of Other Power faith. In the operation of the name of Amida Buddha and his Light, Shinran saw the immediate causes of faith.

The Seventeenth Vow. — According to Shinran, the Seventeenth Vow was the universal source which declared the dissemination of Amida Buddha's name among sentient beings. Although this Vow was one of the forty eight Vows given by that Buddha when he began his striving to save beings, it had never gained an outstandingly prominent place in the teachings of the earlier Pure Land teachers. T'an-luan had taught that the Eighteenth, Eleventh, and Twenty-Second Vows were the central Vows.[29] Shan-tao referred to the Seventeenth Vow in his discussion of deep faith, but he used it only to indicate the fundamental identity of all Buddhist teaching.[30] However, Shinran saw deep spiritual meaning in the Seventeenth Vow that escaped previous teachers. For him it revealed the link between the effect of the fulfillment of Amida Buddha's Vows in the ideal realm and the historical appearance of that teaching in the time-space realm of sentient beings. It provided an absolute basis for the historical tradition.

Attention was drawn to the work of Sakyamuni Buddha because he came into the world in order to reveal the work of Amida Buddha to beings in accordance with the Seventeenth Vow.[31]

[28] See above p. 156 for text of the Vow.
[29] *SSZ.*, I, 9-10.
[30] *Ibid.*
[31] *Ibid.*, II, 43-44.

The proclamation of this teaching by Sakyamuni Buddha was in accord with the original intention for the appearance of a Buddha in the world as stated by Sakyamuni Buddha to Ananda in the *Muryōjukyō*. He declared that a Buddha appears in the world out of the infinite compassion for the beings of the three worlds and out of a deep desire to bestow real benefit on beings.[32] In fulfillment of this intention Sakyamuni Buddha, according to Shinran, taught the *Muryōjukyō, Kammuryōjukyō* and *Amidakyō* which fully revealed the way of salvation established by Amida Buddha and was the basis for Pure Land teaching in India, China and Japan.

By stressing this interpretation of the intention for the appearance of the Buddha in the world, Shinran reversed the traditional relationship between the "Holy Path" and the Pure Land school. In the earlier tradition Pure Land doctrine was considered merely as an expedient way in Buddhism for inferior people. However with Shinran, the "Holy Path" became completely instrumental and subsidiary to the Pure Land teaching. The difficult practices and teachings were expedient doctrines in order to bring finally the devotee to faith in Amida Buddha's Vow.[33]

The titles which Shinran uses to describe the Seventeenth Vow also reveal to us other aspects of the theological importance of this Vow for him. In the *Kyōgyōshinshō* where he discusses the titles of this Vow, two are instructive. On the one hand, he called it "the Vow of the Transfer (of Merit) for Going (to the Pure Land)." On the other hand, he termed it "the Vow of the Selected (practice of) the Recitation of the Name." In the first title he wished to show that the foundation for the Other Power way of salvation was given in this Vow through the declaration of Amida Buddha's way of salvation by all the Buddhas in the universe. In the second title, Shinran taught that the Seventeenth Vow was the true basis for the practice of recitation which had traditionally been based on the phrase Naishi Junen, "till ten thoughts," of the Eighteenth Vow.[34] The significance of his view lies in the fact that the Eighteenth Vow was released from its traditional connotation of the Vow of practice,[35] by distinguishing the Seventeenth Vow as "the Vow of True Practice" i. e. the "Vow in which the Buddhas Recite the Name." The Eighteenth Vow was then designated "the Vow of True Faith" i. e., the "Vow of Sincere Faith." The center of Shinran's interest in the Eighteenth Vow was shifted from the consideration of the practice of that Vow in its traditional sense to the contemplation of the faith that was promised in the Vow.

Through his interpretation of the Seventeenth Vow, Shinran was able to explain the existence and meaning of the Pure Land tradition, and he was

[32] *Ibid.*, I, 4. Shinran's interpretation is given in *Ichinentanenmoni, Ibid.*, II, 614-615, 618.

[33] Umehara, *Kyōgyōshinshō Shinshaku, op. cit.*, I, 39-40.

[34] *SSZ.*, II, 5.

[35] *Ibid.*, 42-43.

able to root the process of the arising of faith in beings to the cosmic process of the realization of Amida Buddha's compassion and desire to save all beings. It was an important concept contributing to the consistency of Shinran's interpretation of Pure Land doctrine.

The Name and Light: The Immediate Causes of Faith. — In tracing Shinran's thought on the way in which Amida Buddha's gift of faith is realized among men, we come now to take up the immediate causes for the arising of faith which he regarded as issuing from Amida Buddha's compassion and finding fulfillment within the human consciousness. In this process he pointed to two factors. The active cause he designated as the name of Amida Buddha and the passive cause he termed the Light of Amida Buddha. His interpretation of this process is mainly philosophical since the name and Light of Amida Buddha are regarded as transcendental realities embodying Amida Buddha's compassion and wisdom.

Shinran's conception of the name of Amida Buddha is rooted in the theory developed in the Pure Land tradition. T'an-luan was the first of the Pure Land patriarchs to present a theory of the name. As we have observed earlier, the name, according to his theory, embodied the total reality of the nature of Amida Buddha. Therefore, when it was repeated, it had the power to cleanse and purify evil beings and to bring them great benefit.[36] Hōnen also formulated a significant conception of the virture of the name which he stated in the *Senjakushu:*

> ...the Nembutsu is superior and all other practices are inferior, because all virtues are wrapt up in the one sacred name. There are the four wisdoms, the three bodies, the ten faculties, the four fearlessnesses, and all other virtues of the inner faculties, external signs, light rays, sermons, the benefitting of others — indeed all outward activities. These, I say, are inherent in the sacred name of the Buddha.[37]

Shinran was also influenced by these ancient ideas concerning names. Nevertheless his use of the idea was quite different from preceding teachers, and his use purged the conception of any magical overtones. He would agree that the name of Amida Buddha contained the whole virtue of the Buddha within itself. But this name and its power were not to be conceived merely in terms of the practice of the recitation done by sentient beings as an effort to gain salvation.

The name as conceived by Shinran is that name, Amida, sounded forth by the Buddhas of the universe in accordance with the Seventeenth Vow. It is the true cause of salvation as it mysteriously arouses faith in sentient beings when they hear it and become aware that it embodies Amida Buddha's compassionate intention to save all beings. Conceived in this manner, the

[36]See the study of T'an-luan above pp.7-11.

[37]Coates and Ishizuka, *op. cit.,* II, 343.

name of Amida is no longer the merely vocal element in the practice of recitation, but it is the mysterious activity of Amida Buddha within the minds of men.

Shinran, thus speaks of the name as the "efficient cause of rebirth."[38] or as a "father"[39] signifying the positive activity of the name in bringing about salvation.

Before moving on to discuss the second factor in the arising of faith we must call attention to an important aspect of the conception of the name. Shinran's understanding of the activity of the name must be considered from both objective and subjective standpoints. The transfer of the name of Amida Buddha to beings as represented by the Seventeenth Vow is the objective aspect. However, when the transfer of the name is analyzed, discussion must move immediately to the subjective aspect. Although the name is spoken of as an objective existence, in reality it only manifests itself as the subjective factor of faith when that faith is expressed in the practice of recitation. The name is thus never separate or apart from beings, but intertwined in their existence as faith or recitation, as the manifestation of faith in mind, word or deed.[40] This is a very difficult point for Westerners to comprehend in Buddhist thought even beyond Shinran's thought. That is, that objective reality appears to be dissolved into the subjective awareness. Frequently fundamental concepts pointing to transcendental realities are described by Buddhists, but they immediately qualify their thought by indicating that the realities that they refer to do not exist outside the mind of the believer as a self-subsisting, objective reality. Rather what is spoken of as apparently existing objectively, because of the way in which men must express their thought, is, in reality, to be discovered within one's consciousness. Hence for Shinran, the name of Amida Buddha is not some metaphysical entity or some objective existence somewhere in the world, nor truly are the Buddhas who speak this name some type of objective existences located in the universe. The name, spoken by the Buddhas, or heard by people in whom the faith is to be aroused, is the name heard upon the lips of ordinary people, or the content of teaching in which Amida Buddha's intention is praised, or even as the historical tradition of the Pure Land itself which has consistently proclaimed Amida Buddha's compassion for men.

The second factor which Shinran singled out in the process of the arising of faith is the Light of Amida Buddha. The Light of the Buddha stands for the aspect of wisdom in a Buddha or a Bodhisattva, and it is usually portrayed in the mythology as a stream of light which illumines every aspect of reality and shows its true nature. The *Muryōjukyō* gives a picture of the Light generated

[38]Suzuki, *Miscellany on the Shin Teaching of Buddhism, op. cit.,* 145.

[39]*SSZ.,* II, 33-34, 694.

[40]Umehara, *Kyōgyōshinshō Shinshaku, op. cit.,* I, 62-63.

by Amida Buddha as the result of the perfection of the austerities which he
carried out.[41]

Amida Buddha's nature as Infinite Light is based on the fulfillment of his
Twelfth Vow[42] in which he promised that there would be no place in the universe which would not be illumined by his Light, that is, his wisdom. Wisdom
in Buddhism means to see things as they really are, to apprehend the true
nature of things and oneself.

The Light of Amida Buddha, as the passive cause for the arising of faith in
men, interpreted by Shinran, refers to that religious experience when the
individual feels himself to be illumined, when the significance and meaning of
the teaching becomes real to him. According to Shinran, the Light of Amida
Buddha is promoting faith in men when "they feel the darkness of Ignorance
gradually fading in them and are ready to see the seed of good karma ger-
minate."[43] The experience of Amida Buddha's Light in his thought was attended by the double insight into the sinful condition of beings and the comple-
mentary insight that trust in Amida Buddha's Vows will result in liberation
from the bonds of finitude.

What we have said above concerning the subjective-objective relation of the
name in Shinran's thought also applied to his conception of the Light of Amida
Buddha. This Light approaches the sense of the "glory" of divinity as perhaps
seen in the beauty or order of nature. However, its function is not to indicate
something of the nature of the universe, but to point directly to man's nature as
a sinner, and to make him aware of the compassion of Amida Buddha. In this
way the Light stimulates men to faith in Amida Buddha's Vows.

In connection with the concept of Light, Shinran developed a theory which
shows again how his sense that salvation is completely the work of Amida
Buddha influenced his treatment of traditional Pure Land themes. He placed
great emphasis on the fact that in the experience of salvation "one is accepted
and protected by unimpeded Light of Amida Buddha's mind."[44] This is the
concept of the "acceptance (by Amida's Light) which does not reject."

One important aspect of Shinran's own spiritual experience was his sense
of being accepted and not abandoned by Amida Buddha. This experience within his consciousness countered his sense of spiritual incapacity and lost-
ness, because he recognized that Amida Buddha was the sole source of salvation. Through this experience, and its formulation into a key doctrine in
his thought, Shinran found strong evidence for his understanding of faith as a
gift of Amida Buddha. According to him, the moment in which faith arises is

---

[41] *Sacred Books of the East*, XLIX, *op. cit.*, 28-30.

[42] See above p. 2.

[43] Suzuki, *Miscellany on the Shin Teaching of Buddhism, op. cit.*, 45.

[44] *SSZ.*, II, 670.

the moment when beings receive Amida Buddha's acceptance. Thus he declared:

> True faith is caused to arise through the efforts of the two Honorables, Sakyamuni Buddha and Amida Buddha. When we say that faith is determined, it means the time when one is given "Acceptance." After that one abides in the status of the company of the truly assured, and it will be so until he is born into the Pure Land.[45]

Through Shinran's frequent reference to the Light of Amida Buddha we could describe his theology as a theology of Light. For according to him it is in the embrace of Light that passion-ridden beings are granted the status of salvation realized in the awakening of faith. On its cognitive side the Light reveals to man his true nature as passion-ridden and shows him the way of faith in Amida Buddha. However, this knowledge is not factual datum, but inner awareness of one's spiritual condition and the simultaneous awareness that in effect Amida Buddha, by fulfillment of his aspirations, has already deigned to save such beings. This is faith itself. On its transcendental side, the embrace of Light points to the fact that the sole ground of salvation is Amida Buddha. Thus Shinran extolled that Light, for as one is illumined by this Light he senses that his sins are cleansed, that karmic bonds are broken, and all illusions are dispelled. Surrounded by Amida Buddha's Light faith grows and there is joy. Thus Shinran calls all men to submit themselves to this Light and share its wondrous blessing;

> Wisdom's light is infinite.
> Of all finite beings, there are none
> That light have not received.
> Let us take refuge in the True Light![46]

Shinran's concept of salvation through the embrace within Amida Buddha's Light represents a significant change in emphasis from the traditional Pure Land doctrine based on his insight into the nature of absolute Other Power. According to previous Pure Land doctrine, the Light of Amida Buddha shone only on those who recite the name. The basis for this view was the *Kammuryōjukyō*:

> Buddha Amitayus has eighty four thousand signs of perfection, each sign is possessed of eighty-four minor marks of excellence, each mark has eighty-four thousand rays, each ray extends so far as to shine over the world of the ten quarters, whereby Buddha embraces and protects all beings who think upon him and does not exclude (any of them).[47]

---

[45] *Ibid.*, 673-674. See also 678-679.
[46] *Ibid.*, 486.

[47] *SBE.*, LXIX, *op. cit.*, 180. *SSZ.*, I, 57.

Shan-tao's interpretation of the text makes it clear that to think on the Buddha means to recite Amida Buddha's name. He shows also that the degree of spiritual benefit of the practice is directly dependent on the intensity and constancy of the devotee's effort.[48] He stresses the fact that the illumination of the Buddha is attained only by those who think on Amida Buddha's name and not by those who employ other practices or devote themselves to other Buddhas.[49]

The concept of Amida Buddha's Light in traditional Pure Land thought was connected entirely with the merit acquiring process, and was received as a result of intense spiritual endeavor in the practice of the recitation of the Buddha's name. Thus experience assured the devotee of his union with the Buddha and no doubt was an experience of great spiritual depth.

It can readily be seen that Shinran differed sharply from this narrow understanding of Amida Buddha's Light which restricted its operation to only an effect of discipline. For Shinran, the idea was elevated to a cosmic or universal level as the precondition for the salvation of all beings. For him it was the spiritual basis whereby the Buddha acted to make known to beings their sinful and degenerate condition and to assure them of his compassionate intention in his Vow. In other words the Light, as understood by Shinran, was the source or cause of faith, rather than the visionary effect of meditative discipline.

We bring our discussion of the two causes of the arising of faith in beings to an end by stating that the function of these two concepts, the name and Light of Amida Buddha, is to give further support to Shinran's theory that salvation comes about entirely through the work of Amida Buddha. In order to substantiate this insight, Shinran had to develop these concepts in his distinctive manner to indicate the universal process through which faith is realized in beings.

Further, the Seventeenth Vow establishes the connection which explains the emergence of Amida Buddha's salvation into the historical world, while the name and Light serve to establish the connection between Amida Buddha's compassionate activity and the experience of faith in the individual.

Conversion.—We have pointed out that the activity of the name and the Light relate primarily to the experience of faith in the individual. The idea that faith is a gift of Amida Buddha and also the understanding that it arises and is manifested when a man is aware of his sinful state and the availability of the Buddha's compassion, both point to the fact that there must be a decisive time when this salvation is effected. In other words there is a concept of conversion in Shinran's thought. This concept of conversion will naturally reflect his own experience as he achieved this insight under the tutelage of Hōnen and thereby put an end to futile religious striving. The concept of conversion as developed by Shinran is completely consistent with his under-

---

[48]*SSZ.*, I, 521-522.   [49]*Ibid.*, 628-629.

standing that salvation comes about through the work of Amida Buddha. Conversion is not a matter of human effort.

Shinran's concept of conversion is based on the term Ōchō, translated as transverse transcendence. In our discussion of the term Ō (横)[50] we pointed out that it implied an instantaneous achievement of salvation, which meant that no human contrivance was involved. In the *Songōshinzōmeimon* he wrote that "since one has attained faith, therefore, we must know that we have transversely cut off the five evil paths. As for the term Ōchō, Ō speaks of the Tathagata's Vow Power, Other Power. Chō (超) signifies that we pass over the sea of births and deaths easily and enter the capital of the unsurpassed great Nirvana."[51]

In a similar vein, Shinran employed the term Eshin (回心) which may be translated as "turning the mind" and is taken as the conversion experience itself. According to Shinran, conversion means to reverse the mind of self power. That is to reject the way of works, good deeds, purifying exercises, and turn in faith to Amida Buddha's Vow.[52]

In both terms Ōchō and Eshin the aspect of discontinuity which occurs at the moment of the arising of faith was interpreted by Shinran as the result of the activity of Amida Buddha, and this activity was manifested in the individual's experience as the rejection of self effort and reliance on the Buddha. Thus it was a decisive experience which took place once and for all.[53]

Shinran's understanding of conversion permitted him to give a deeper theological basis for the religious life. Following the critical classification of doctrines in the Tandai school, he maintained that faith in Amida Buddha conferred upon the devotee immediate and total salvation. Thus for him the Pure Land doctrine was the ultimate of Mahayana doctrine because it promised the sudden, instantaneous, complete and perfect salvation which was the ideal of Buddhist tradition. We must turn our attention next to this status which the devotee received in this life as he attained faith in Amida Buddha.

---

[50] See above p. 50-51.

[51] *SSZ.*, II, 562, 576. Also 632.

[52] *Ibid.*, 628.

[53] *Ibid.*, 787-788. According to Yuiembo, conversion occurs only once.

VI

SALVATION NOW!
THE STATUS OF THE
BELIEVER IN PRESENT LIFE

As we have already noted, Shinran gave new meaning to the common life of the devotee which had not been explored or clearly stated in earlier Pure Land teaching. As a result of his insight that faith was a gift and that salvation was entirely dependent on the work of Amida Buddha without any self-assertion on the part of man, he taught that the believer could achieve an assurance of his ultimate salvation in this life. The futuristic emphasis that had dominated Pure Land thought was transformed by Shinran to stress the attainment of salvation in this life. The doctrine in which he clarified this point was his reinterpretation of the traditional idea of "entrance into the company of the truly assured," i.e., those truly assured that they would gain enlightenment.[1] It was also regarded as the achievement of the stage of nonretrogression, a stage in the Bodhisattva path which signified that the Bodhisattva would never fall back into the paths of evil births or karma, and that he was certain to gain the goal of Buddhahood. The concept, as set forth by Shinran, was intimately connected with the ideas of the embrace of Light and the activity of the name, because it was a result of these influences, giving rise to faith, that men were enabled to enter into the company of the truly assured.[2]

The content of the concepts of entrance into the company of the truly assured and the achievement of the stage of non-retrogression does not in itself significantly differ in Shinran from that taught by traditional Pure Land teachers. It was in connection with the temporal relationship of these states to birth in the Pure Land that Shinran manifested his own original insight. Attainment of this ineffable spiritual status occurred at the moment of the arising of faith, according to him:

> ...We say that we abide in the rank of the company of the truly assured when we encounter the profound Vow of the gift[3] of Amida's Other Power and our

---

[1] Translated "Right Established State" in Kosho Yamamoto's work.

[2] *SSZ.*, II, 43, 666-667, 785.

[3] Amida Buddha's transfer of merit (Ekō).

minds which rejoice at being given true faith are assured, and when, because we are accepted by him, we have the adamantine mind.[4]

He also wrote:

Since one remains in the state of non-retrogression until he is born into the Pure Land, (his state) is referred to as "the rank of the company of the truly assured."[5]

He would frequently remind his disciples:

You must all consider that your birth (into the Pure Land) is determined.[6]

The contrast of Shinran's teaching on this point with the traditional masters is clear. The doctrine itself is based on the declaration of Amida Buddha in the Eleventh Vow given in the *Muryōjukyō:*

If those who are born in my country, after my attaining Buddhahood, should not be definitely settled in the group of the faithful before their entrance into Nirvana, may I not attain the Highest Enlightenment.[7]

According to the Vow itself, the entrance into the company of the truly assured takes place with one's birth into the Pure Land. This point is further clarified in the passage on the perfection of the Vow in the same sutra:

Buddha declared to Ananda: "Of the beings who are born into that country, all of them abide in the company of the truly assured. Why? Because in that Buddha land there are none belonging to evil or unassured groups."[8]

Further, the *Amidakyō* also speaks of the fact that the stage of nonretrogression is to be attained in the Pure Land:

Further, Sariputra, in the Land of Bliss, beings born there all are in the state of non-retrogression.[9]

The futuristic emphasis was set forth by T'an-luan the first popularizer of Pure Land teaching in China. He insisted on the principle that the achievement of the state of non-retrogression and enlightenment came about after the rebirth in the Pure Land when the conditions would be right for the mediocre mortal to perform the Bodhisattva disciplines.

[4] *Ibid.*, 684.
[5] *Ibid.*, 674.
[6] *Ibid.*, 689.
[7] Suzuki, *Miscellany on the Shin Teaching of Buddhism, op. cit.,* 15. *SSZ.,* II, *op. cit.,* 9.
[8] *SSZ.,* I, 24.
[9] *Ibid.*, 69.

Shinran's contribution to this teaching was made when he regarded the one moment of faith in this life as determining once and for all the destiny of the individual. He stressed the present moment in order to overcome the anxiety resulting from the moralistic conception of the practice of recitation of the Buddha's name.

A decisive indication of Shinran's departure from the tradition in regard to the nature of salvation is his treatment of the doctrine of Raigo which refers to the promise of the Nineteenth Vow that the Buddha would come at the moment of death to welcome the devotee to the Pure Land. However, the promise depended on the state of mind of the believer in that moment. He had to have a clear and steady mind in order to be thinking deeply on the Buddha. Considerable anxiety arose among the common people as to how they could be sure to have this mind at the point of death. The anxiety is succinctly stated in the *Anjinketsujōsho*:

> The nembutsu as practised by the jiriki followers puts the Buddha away from themselves far in the West, and thinking that they are worthless beings they would now and then recollect the Original Vow of the Buddha and pronounce his Name (shōmyō). This being so the most intimate relationship between the Buddha and all beings fails to establish itself here... Inasmuch as they are common mortals, it is only on exceptional occasions that they cherish pious feelings; and thus they naturally have an uncertain state of mind until the time actually comes for them to depart from this life. While they occasionally pronounce the Name with their mouths, they have no definite assurance for the Pure Land. This position is like that of a feudal retainer who only occasionally comes out in the presence of the lord. His relationship with the latter can never be intimate and trustful. Such a devotee is all the time in an unsettled state of mind as to how to court the favor of the Buddha, how to be reconciled to Him, how to win his loving consideration, and this very fact of his uncertainties alienates him from Buddha, resulting in the unharmonious relationship between the devotee's unsettled mind and Buddha's great compassionate heart. The (jiriki) devotee thus puts himself at a distance from Buddha. As long as he keeps up this attitude of mind his rebirth in the Pure Land is indeed extremely uncertain.[10]

It was widely recognized within the Pure Land school that selfgenerated faith could wax and wane depending on the condition of one's mind. In order to meet the anxieties arising from the uncertainties of this form of faith, Hōnen had taught that the three mental attitudes taught in the *Kammuryō-jukyō* would naturally arise during the process of recitation. Therefore one need not be concerned for their actual conscious appearance. However, as we have already indicated above, Hōnen's thought did not overcome entirely the anxiety arising from the merit acquiring principle.[11]

---

[10]Suzuki, *Miscellany on the Shin Teaching of Buddhism, op. cit.,* 26-27. Jiriki in this passage means Self Power.

[11]See above pp. 21, 22.

Shinran transcended this uncertainty concerning salvation by his assertion that faith is a gift and the individual's salvation lay in the acceptance of Amida Buddha which took form as undoubting faith in the believer. This standpoint ruled out all chance occurrences which might obstruct the individual's ultimate salvation.

Suzuki describes this view:

> The tariki on the other hand places great stress on the significance of the eighteenth Vow made by Amida, and teaches that when the significance of this Vow is fully realized, rebirth is assured and the devotee is released from all worries arising from the sense of separation.[12]

In order to support his striking and novel theory that salvation is absolutely assured in the present life, Shinran called attention to the term Soku (即 Sunawachi). This word in the Chinese text serves as a type of conjunction indicating that what follows comes as a result of the foregoing: In such a case, it can be translated as "therefore" or "then," However, whenever Shinran interpreted the term, he understood it grammatically as a kind of "equals" sign. Employing the word in this latter sense, he was able to make the texts teach that birth in the Pure Land and enlightenment were guaranteed in the present moment of faith. In the *Yuishinshōmoni*, he applies this interpretation to a text of the *Muryōjukyo*:

> In the *Daikyō (Muryōjukyō)* it says: "Those desiring birth in that land (therefore) attain birth (there) and abide in the state of non-retrogression." Ganshō-hikoku (願生彼国) means "one aspires to be born in that country." Sokutokuōjō (即得往生) means that since one attains faith, therefore he is reborn. "Therefore he is reborn" means that he abides in the state of non-retrogression. To abide in the state of non-retrogression means, namely, that it is determined that one is in the rank of the company of the truly assured. It is also called Jōtōshōkaku (上等正覚) "to be (in the state) equivalent to right enlightenment." This is what we mean by "therefore he attains rebirth." Soku (即) is Sunawachi. Sunawachi means that no time elapses, no days intervene.[13]

With this thought of entrance into the company of the truly assured in this life, Shinran attempted to combine the emphasis on the present realization of the fruits of Buddhahood in Nagarjuna's and Vasubandhu's thought and the future attainment of birth in the Pure Land stressed by T'an-luan. He may also have been influenced in his thought by the contemporary stress of the Tendai and Shingon schools which proclaimed the possibility of attaining Buddhahood in this life (Sokushinjōbutsu). However Shinran gave a peculiarly

[12] Suzuki, *Miscellany on the Shin Teaching of Buddhism, op. cit.*, 27.

[13] *SSZ.*, II, 625. Also 538, 605, 617-618. Notice the analysis of the term Soku-i (即位) in the investiture of the crown prince. Shinran may have gotten his interpretation of Soku from such terms as Nehan soku Shōji which is Nirvana is Samsara.

Pure Land interpretation to this doctrine which was normally associated with the self power, purifying practices of the Holy Path tradition of Buddhism.

Because of the degree of similarity of Shinran's teaching and that of the contemporary schools on this point, his letters reflect the confusion of his disciples as they tried to distinguish the absolute Other Power view from the traditional self power view. Shinran made it clear that his view was entirely based on Other Power and must not in any way be transformed into a basis for self power activity.[14]

The confusion which developed about this doctrine in Shinran's thought may have arisen from the fact that Bodhisattva Miroku was portrayed as attaining the status of Buddhahood in the sutras through self power disciplines. When Shinran employed this figure, he may have been understood to be emphasizing the self power aspect also. However, his intention in using the figure was to point out clearly that Miroku, though a Bodhisattva, had performed austerities sufficient to *assure* that he would become Buddha in his next life. Hence he is already called Miroku Buddha. That is, he is regarded as equal to a Buddha although his attainment is yet in the future.[15]

While Shinran stressed the fact that it was a certainty that Bodhisattva Miroku would become Buddha, he contrasted the self power way of the Boddhisattva with the Other Power way taught in the Pure Land school. Like Bodhisattva Miroku, he declared, believers in Amida Buddha are in a state of cause with respect to Buddhahood. That is, the cause is perfected presently, but its realization takes place in the immediate future. Shinran also pointed out the contrast that Miroku's attainment comes after millions of years of austerities. Thus his attainment falls into the category of the "Gradual" which in the critical classification of doctrine of Tendai Shinran points to a lower form of Buddhist teaching. However, he declared that his teaching was the ultimate of the instantaneous teachings because enlightenment comes immediately upon the passing of the individual in death.[16] By way of illustration he referred to the growth of the Kokenju tree which rises about a thousand feet in one day. This is the Pure Land way. In contrast, the pine tree grows very slowly and represents the self power way.[17]

Shinran, thus, made it clear that believers are equal to Bodhisattva Miroku in terms of the goal they approach, but they do not, however, travel the same path to get there. The comparison is based on the *certainty* and the *assurance* of attainment, and the contrast is founded on the difference in the modes of attainment, as self power or Other Power.

After establishing the fact that salvation is assured in this life, Shinran takes up the glorious character of this status which the believer receives. In both

---

[14]*Ibid.*, 681.
[15]*Ibid.*, 684.

[16]*Ibid.*, 678.
[17]*Ibid.*

prose and poetry, he declares the wonderful blessings of this new religious existence. To amplify the meaning of this state, he employed a variety of metaphors. We have already observed that the believer is compared to Bodhisattva Miroku, or said to be equal to the Buddha himself or to be in a state equivalent to true enlightenment.[18] The intimate relation of the devotee and the Buddha is depicted in such terms as "the true Buddhist disciple"[19] or the close and dear friend of the Buddha.[20] The praises which the Buddhas direct toward Amida according to the Seventeenth Vow are also directed to believers.[21] No adjective can express the superior virtue of such people.[22] In the word of the *Kammuryōjukyō,* the believer is a lotus among men. In Buddhist metaphor the lotus is the symbol of the highest Buddhist ideals.[23]

The person established in faith and joined in the company of the truly assured leads a life marked by joy. To be equal with the Buddhas and experience the acceptance of Amida Buddha means that one has attained the stage of joy which is the first of the ten stages in the course of a Bodhisattva.[24]

An important aspect of Shinran's religious experience was the deep sense of joy and gratitude which welled up within him as he reflected on the compassion and mercy he had received from Amida Buddha. Joy and gratitude became for him the outstanding traits of the life of faith. In a variety of passages he expressed his own joy and gratitude such as we find in the epilogue of the *Kyōgyōshinshō* after he recounted the circumstances of his conversion and relation to Hōnen:

> O how happy I am. My mind is established on the Buddha land of the profound Vow. My thought is set afloat on the sea of the Inconceivable doctrine. I have experienced the Tathagata's compassion (Amida Buddha's) deeply, and I sincerely cherish the kindness of my teacher. Happiness abounds, reverence grows deeper, because here are gathered the teachings of Shinshū[25] and the essentials of the Pure Land are manifested. I am only mindful of the depth of Buddha's grace, and I am not ashamed at the ridicule of men.[26]

The joy of faith is characterized by dancing or leaping for joy (Yuyaku 踊躍) in heaven and on earth.[27]

In addition to the spiritual joy which results from acceptance by Amida Buddha Shinran listed ten blessings which are also given to those attaining true faith:

---

[18] *Ibid.,* 574-575, 600, 607, 661, 666-667.

[19] *Ibid.,* 75, 660.

[20] *Ibid.,* 684.

[21] *Ibid.,* 662-663.

[22] *Ibid.,* 660.

[23] *Ibid.,* I, 66; II, 608.

[24] Yamamoto, *op. cit.,* 452.

[25] Shinshū refers to True Teaching, True Sect (of the Pure Land).

[26] *SSZ.,* II, 202-203.

[27] *Ibid.,* 633.

Those who have attained the adamantine true mind transcend the five destinies[28] and the eight difficulties,[29] and they attain assuredly in this life ten blessings. What are these ten? One is the blessing of the protection of spiritual power: two, possession of highest virtue; three, the blessing of transforming evil into good; four, protection of all the Buddhas; five, the blessing of being praised by all Buddhas; six, always protected by the light of the mind (of the Buddhas); seven, the blessing of always having a joyous mind; eight, the blessing of being mindful of the grace (of the Buddha) and requiting virtue; nine, always practicing great mercy; ten, the blessing of entrance into the company of the truly assured.[30]

In a poem entitled *Genzeiryakuwasan,* Shinran also declared the benefits to be gained in this life through faith in Amida Buddha. The chief theme which he expressed was the fact that those who praise Amida Buddha's name enjoy the spiritual protection of all the Buddhas, gods and spirits:

> Faith that results from the mystery of the Vow power
> Is the great mind of Bodhi (Enlightenment).
> The evil demons that fill heaven and earth
> All fear it togeather.
> . . .
>
> Within the light of the Buddha of Unimpeded Light
> Infinite Amida Buddhas abide.
> Transformed Buddhas, each together,
> Protect (those of) true faith.[31]

The spiritual character of this power and protection of Amida Buddha is expressed by Shinran when he declares the superiority of the Pure Land way:

> The Nembutsu (Pure Land teaching) is the unimpeded single way. If one asks the reason, it is because the spirits of heaven and earth submit reverently to the devotee of faith. The world of evil spirits and heretical teachings never obstruct, and they (devotees) do not experience the consequences of sins, good deeds, though many, never surpass (the effectiveness of the Nembutsu or faith).[32]

It is to be especially observed that Shinran stressed primarily the spiritual aspects of the Buddha's blessings. The Shinshū community, based on Shinran's teaching, avoided the more magical and superstitious practices used by other sects to gain and hold followers.[33]

---

[28] Soothill and Hodous, *op. cit.,* 127b. The five destinies (skt. gati) are birth in a hell, as a hungry ghost, animal, human being, or god.

[29] *Ibid.,* 41a refers to the eight hindrances to seeing a Buddha. These are listed as a birth in a hell, as a hungry ghost, birth in the land of Uttarakuru, a pleasant region to the north, birth in a heaven where life is easy, as deaf, dumb or blind, and as a worldly philosopher in the time when there is no Buddha.

[30] *Ibid.,* 72.

[31] *Ibid.,* 498-499.

[32] *Ibid.,* 777.

[33] See A. I. Reischauer, "A Catechism of the Shin Sect," *Transactions of the Asiatic Society of Japan,* Vol. XXXVIII. Part V, 333-395. See also Mitsuyuki Ishida, *Path of the Buddha, op. cit.,* 335.

Our study of the status of the believer in the present life indicates that Shinran gave a far reaching reinterpretation of the way of salvation through faith in Amida Buddha. While he continued to maintain that the final realization of enlightenment took place upon birth in the Pure Land after death, he focused attention on the spiritual nature of present existence. This was the sphere in which salvation became assured and certain. The moment of faith was the supreme moment in life and for all intents and purposes may be regarded as the last moment of life for birth in the Pure Land became a certainty. Shinran's view did away with the moralism implied in the traditional view of the last moment of life as well as the anxiety concerning the birth in Pure Land felt by devotees of the way of self power. Through his interpretation he gave new significance to the common life. Now the believer had a spiritual status equal to the Buddha and though he continued to possess a finite sinful nature, he need have no fears concerning his ultimate attainment of enlightenment. The fact that the believer's future destiny was once and for all assured permitted the individual to accept himself as he was and to give up all extraneous and difficult religious practices. As we shall see, the focus of the believer's religious practice and spiritual ideals shifted from the concern to gain salvation for himself to a concern to repay his obligation to the Buddha and to bring others within the sphere of the Buddha's compassion.

VII
FAITH'S EXPRESSION

Shinran's reinterpretation of the way of salvation in the Pure Land school naturally gave rise to a new concept of religious devotion. Within the context of faith as a gift and the present assurance of salvation in this life, all practices and methods of securing salvation through acquiring merit became useless. However, Shinran, as we shall see, did not believe that the spiritual life could be a totally formless existence. Rather he retained the practice of the recitation of Amida Buddha's name which had been the central means for securing salvation in the traditional Pure Land school, but regarded this practice, and any other spiritual activity, as an expression of gratitude on the part of the devotee for the salvation granted by Amida Buddha.

In order to illuminate the creative understanding of Shinran in respect to religious devotion, we shall briefly survey the traditional concept. Based on the teaching of the *Kammuryōjukyō,* the Pure Land school from the time of T'an-luan onward declared that the most evil person "on the strength of (his merit of) uttering the Buddha's name he will, during every repetition, expiate the sins which involve him in births and deaths during eighty millions of kalpas."[1] Also the *Amidakyō* promised that:

> ...if a good man or a good woman, hearing of (Amida) Buddha, holds the Name for one day, two days, three days, four days, five days, six days, or seven days with the thought undisturbed, (Amida) Buddha, accompanied by his holy ones, will appear before such a one at the moment of departing from this life. As the end of life comes and as the mind remains undisturbed, such a one will instantly be born in the country of the Highest Happiness of (Amida) Buddha.[2]

Pure Land teachers followed T'an-luan in the view that the recitation of the name was the chief means of salvation available to ordinary mortals for whom the practices of purification and meditation were too difficult. According to Shan-tao and Genshin this practice had been given because of the weakness

---

[1] *Sacred Books of the East,* XLIX, *op. cit.,* 198.

[2] *SSZ.,* I, 103. To hold the name (Shuji Myōgo) is generally to be understood as reciting the name of Buddha. It was so regarded by Shinran when he defined rebirth according to the *Amidakyō.* See *SSZ.,* II, 557-558.

of ordinary people. They maintained that "their mind is coarse. Consciousness flounders; the mind flies."[3] Hōnen brought this teaching to its clearest expression when he asserted that the recitation was the ultimate practice for gaining salvation.[4] Many examples of the thought of this school can be drawn from the *Kyōgyōshinshō* in the volume on practice where Shinran gathered passages to exalt the practice of the recitation of the name.[5]

Although the validity of the recitation of the tradition rested in the virtue resident in the name of Amida Buddha, Shinran directed this virtue toward the event of the awakening of faith, rather than toward the achievement of rebirth through the recitation of the name. While he followed tradition in the theory that the name of Amida Buddha was the basis for birth in the Pure Land, he did not connect it to the finite repetition by mortals, but to the universal recitation of the name carried out by all Buddhas according to the Seventeenth Vow.

Shinran's view of this practice in the *Kyōgyōshinshō* shows some interesting variation from the traditional viewpoint. The great practice of which he writes has two aspects. On the one hand, it is the great practice of the Buddhas which comes about as the fulfillment of the Seventeenth Vow. On the other hand, the great practice also refers to the recitation of the name by devotees. When Shinran discusses the recitation of the name performed by devotees, it is noticeable that he shifts attention from the act of recitation and its virtue, to the name which points to the ultimate source of virtue of the practice. He stressed the fact that the recitation of the name " . . . is not a self power practice of people and sages. Therefore we say that it is a discipline in which one does not transfer the merit (Fuekō). Sages of Mahayana or Hinayana, and persons with a heavy burden or a light burden of sin, all, similarly, must take refuge in the selected, great jewelled sea and become Buddha through the Nembutsu (The Pure Land way)."[6]

The recitation which is the cause of salvation for Shinran is *not practised by individuals for their own salvation.* The practice that brings salvation is that performed by the Buddha, and it is heard by the beings in the universe. As a result of their hearing that name and through the illumination of Amida Buddha's Light, the inner cause of faith is aroused.

While Shinran declared to his disciples that the practice of recitation was the central teaching he had received from Hōnen,[7] he evidences advance over Hōnen in distinguishing decisively between the self power recitation of the name and that of true Other Power. Thus, as we shall see, he retained the practice, but altered its meaning.

The self power method of recitation "is when the devotee recites the names of various Buddhas according to respective situations and practices the various

---

[3] *SSZ.,* II, 19.   [5] *SSZ.,* II, 5-46.   [7] *Ibid.,* 773-774.
[4] DeBary, *op. cit.,* 208.   [6] *Ibid.,* 33.

roots of good, and thinks that he will be reborn into the Pure Land by relying on himself and with a mind of self effort to adjust the confusion of his body, mouth and mind to end life auspiciously."[8] Such people have a definitely futuristic conception of birth in the Pure Land and they are acutely concerned with the problem of the last moment of life.[9]

Shinran, however, was unequivocal in stating that he rejected completely a self power practice in any form. Thus on one occasion he declared to his disciples:

> Since you believe that it is inconceivable (mysterious), you should not contrive with this or that. *The deeds for rebirth (into the Pure Land) are not our efforts...* You should entrust yourself only to Tathagata (Amida Buddha)...[10]

This point is further elaborated in the Tannishō:

> Nembutsu is neither a practice nor a good (deed) for the devotee. Since we do not practice it by our own contrivance we say it is non-practice. Also, since it is not a good (deed) which we do by our own contrivance we say it is non-good. Since we leave off the self power and earnestly accord with Other Power, (we say) it is non-practice and non-good for the devotee.[11]

The final rejection of the self power recitation was given by Shinran even at the risk of being accused of not fulfilling his duty of filial piety.[12]

Shinran's viewpoint concerning the rejection of the self power recitation was taken up by his successors such as Yuiembo and Rennyo. Yuiembo flatly denied the traditional theory that a single recitation cleanses from sins sufficient to release a person from eight billion years in hell.[13] Rennyo also rejected the self power practice whereby people believe happiness comes by mechanically reciting the name.[14]

It is clear in Shinran's teaching that, while the practice was not the root cause of salvation, faith was manifest in, or through, the practice of recitation. In several passages he linked practice and faith.[15]

> Even though there is both the one moment of faith (Shin no ichinen) and the one thought of practice (Gyō no ichinen), there is no practice separate from faith and there is no "one moment" of faith separate from the one thought of practice. The reason is that what we call practice is to do the "ten thoughts (Junen)" or to recite vocally as we hear that we attain rebirth (in the Pure Land) by vocally reciting the name of (Amida Buddha given in) the Original Vow. As we say that the one moment of faith is to hear the Vow without the slightest doubt in our minds, we hear that there is no faith apart from practice because we do not understand that there is no practice apart from faith. You must be aware that all of these refer to Amida Buddha's Vow. Practice and faith speak of his Vow.[16]

[8]*Ibid.*, 658.

[9]*Ibid.*, 656.

[10]*Ibid.*, 670.

[11]*Ibid.*, 777.

[12]See above p. 30.

[13]*SSZ.*, 785-786.

[14]Yamamoto, *op. cit.*, 289.

[15]*SSZ.*, II, 5. Also 174; 33; 175; 34.

[16]*Ibid.*, 671-672.

Although Shinran declared that faith and practice were inseparable, it is faith that renders the recitation meaningful. The practice is essentially the expression of faith. The urge to repeat the name is contingent on the arising of faith. In the religious experience the two aspects appear simultaneously. Shinran is quoted to this effect in the *Tannishō:*

> In the moment that we believe that we gain rebirth (in the Pure Land), being saved through the mystery of the Vow of Amida Buddha, and there arises in our minds the thought to recite (say) the name of (Nembutsu), we are then given the blessing of the acceptance and non-rejection of (Amida Buddha).[17]

It is Shinran's firm conviction that "one says the name (Nembutsu) when he is aroused by Amida Buddha (when he receives the urge, or inspiration of Amida Buddha.)"[18]

Shinran's treatment of the Eighteenth Vow also indicates the priority of faith over practice in his thought. He called this Vow the "Vow of Sincere Faith." As he interpreted it, the phrase "until ten thoughts" (naishi jūnen) which traditionally had been the central focus of attention became secondary to the fact of faith and its result. It is also interesting to note here that he interpreted the character Nen (念.   thought) as indicating faith. He wrote:

> Nen signifies that one believes without a double mind Tathagata's Vow.[19]

In addition he interpreted the phrase Tannembutsu which might ordinarily mean "many Nembutsu" or "Multiple Recitation" to mean a great mind, a superior mind, an unsurpassed mind, of faith which was attained in the conversion from the self power attitude to the Other Power.[20] This identification of faith and the practice of recitation is further strengthened by his declaration:

> When one believes singleheartedly in the Vow of Rebirth through recitation (Nembutsu) without having two minds (i.e., a wavering mind), we call it the "Singlehearted, sole practice (of Nembutsu)."[21]

In Rennyo's thought also the practice of recitation became merged with faith and its nature as mere vocalization was completely transcended:

> Faith is none other but what is contained in these six letters...Therefore we feel all the more that what these six letters "Namuamidabutsu" manifest to us is the way by which we get born into the Pure Land. This being the case, though we say "Anjin" or Shinjin," all after all amount to faith in what is manifested in these six letters of His Name. Anybody with this faith is called one who has attained the Great Faith of the Other Power.[22]

---

[17] *Ibid.*, 773.   [19] *Ibid.*, 628.   [21] *Ibid.*, 693.
[18] *Ibid.*, 776.   [20] *Ibid.*   [22] Yamamoto, *op. cit.*, 297-298.

In the faith volume of the *Kyōgyōshinshō* Shinran states that "true faith inevitably provides the name, but the name does not assuredly provide the faith of the Vow Power."[23] By this he intended to show that the central element in the true practice of recitation was faith. The mere recitation itself was insufficient unless it was inspired by a deep trust in Amida Buddha's Vow. It is the faith, not the practice of recitation, which is the cause of birth in the Pure Land. This point was made explicit in the *Shōshinge* when he stated that "the name of the Original Vow is the Right Determined Act; the Vow of Sincere faith is the *cause*."[24]

It has become clear in our study that Shinran accepted the traditional practice of recitation, and then proceeded to give it a reinterpretation along the lines of his concept of absolute Other Power. Practice ceased to be a purely mechanical, vocal means of gaining birth and a source of spiritual pride in keeping the record of the number said in one day. Rather it became for him a sign of praise and gratitude in which the devotee acknowledged his great debt to Amida Buddha.

The theme of gratitude runs through Shinran's thought. The experience of faith, assurance of salvation and the deep spiritual joy which he had received in his own life made him ever conscious of his great obligation to the Buddhas, Amida and Sakyamuni, and to his teachers whose writings had contributed to his insight:

> We must repay the grace of Tathāgata's great compassion,
> Though our bodies are (ground) to powder.
> The grace of the masters and teachers also we must repay,
> Though our bones be crushed.[25]

Yuiembo, Shinran's disciple, has recorded Shinran's eloquent confession of gratitude for his salvation in the *Tannishō*:

> When I consider well the Vow upon which Amida Buddha thought for five aeons, (I reflect) it was for me Shinran alone. O how grateful I am for the Original Vow which aspired to save one who possesses such evil karma.[26]

This sense of gratitude permeates his writings and is particularly reflected in the *Kyōgyōshinshō* and his poetry.[27]

Just as Shinran was constantly mindful of his own obligation to the Buddha and his teachers, he frequently reminded his followers that they also should keep before them the debt they owed; particularly when they were tempted to defame the gods and Buddhas, or when faced with opposition.[28]

---

[23] *SSZ.*, II, 68.
[24] *Ibid.*, 43.
[25] *Ibid.*, 523.

[26] *Ibid.*, 792.
[27] *Ibid.*, 43, 166, 203, 491, 520, 522.
[28] *Ibid.*, 660, 710.

It was his conviction that gratitude was the direct expression of faith and when faith blossomed in the Vow there would be an outpouring of thankfulness to the Buddha and all the good teachers who made the way possible.[29]

From among Shinran's many statements concerning the expression of gratitude, it is clear that the chief and supreme way is to recite the name of Amida Buddha:

> Only by constantly reciting the Tathagata's name
> Can we repay the grace of the Vow of great compassion.[30]

The theme of gratitude was taken up by Yuiembo, Zonkaku and Rennyo who were leaders in interpreting Shinran's thought. In consequence of the emphasis on gratitude, this trait became a distinctive characteristic of the Shinshū view of life.

To point out the centrality of gratitude to Buddha in Shinshū faith is not to deny that other Buddhists also express gratitude to the Buddha. Shan-tao had written earlier that the followers of self power were not likely to be grateful, but that a follower of Amida Buddha would acknowledge his debt.[31] It is also well known that gratitude and repayment of obligation is a fundamental aspect of Japanese culture which immediately strikes the eye of even the most casual observer. The significant point concerning the Shinshū view is that it became the central function of the religious life and practice. All utilitarianism, magic and attempts to gain some private benefit from religion, were rejected. It was a bold attempt to reduce the egocentrism and legalism that had dominated Pure Land tradition in its quest of salvation for the common man.

Gratitude as a way of life in Shinshū extends beyond the physical or mental practice of recitation. It also penetrates other areas such as ethic and morality. In texts referred to earlier we have noted that awareness of Buddha's grace should prevent true believers from speaking ill of others, of other sects and divinities. Rather it should inspire sympathy and pity.

It must be pointed out here that Shinran was not intent on presenting an ethical system, though he does give counsel on problems of conduct that arose among his disciples.[32] He is also credited with the formation of a document of ethical injunctions in twenty-one rules of conduct.[33] It was Rennyo, however, who gave the theoretical formulation to Shinshū ethics as it has been practised up to the present day in his theory of two levels of truth as applied to ethics. In this theory the Shinshū believer obeys the conventional morality although in

---

[29] *Ibid.*, 777.

[30] *Ibid.*, 44. Also 519.

[31] *Ibid.*, 165.

[32] *Ibid.*, 691.

[33] Akamatsu, *Kamakura Bukkyō no Kenkyū, op. cit.*, 120-124. Akamatsu, *Shinran Zenshu, op. cit.*, II, 7. Hisao Tanaka, *Ibid.*, 178.

his mind he is free because his destiny is determined through faith in Amida Buddha. Rennyo also provided ethical admonitions.[34]

Shinran provided the guideline that everything must be done in respect of that obligation which one has toward the Buddha. The radical nature of his teaching concerning the evil man as the prime object of Amida Buddha's work of salvation, and the instruction that those with faith should not put on the appearance of wisdom, or undertake purifying practices in repentance for their sins, was misunderstood by some disciples to mean that the believer should not be concerned about his behavior. They applied a radical theological concept to their practical ethical lives in a manner which brought disrepute to the doctrine. Shinran declared that it was irrational to take poison merely because one has an antidote for it. He recognized the eternal propensity of man to sin, but he rejected the idea that the evil man was justified in sinning consciously.

---

[34]Yamamoto, *op. cit.,* 311.

VIII

THE BELIEVER'S DESTINY

Shinran's understanding of the final destiny of sentient beings generally followed the traditional teaching of the Pure Land school. However, he interpreted this doctrine in line with his effort to emphasize the absolute Other Power principle and to eliminate ego centrism from religion.

In explaining his thought, we must call attention to the developments which had taken place in the Pure Land tradition. In the Pure Land school the goal of the Pure Land symbolized the ultimate goal of Nirvana sought by all Buddhists. As Mahayana Buddhism evolved, it became apparent that not all individuals had the same capacity for arousing faith and undertaking religious disciplines. Accordingly, it was taught that the Buddha had adapted his teaching to meet the various abilities of his hearers out of his deep compassion and wisdom.

The Pure Land sutras which are the fundamental texts of this tradition were undoubtedly formulated with the awareness of the variant capacities of beings and with a desire to make Buddha's compassion available to all beings. The mythological presentation of the Pure Land with its various qualities and the gradations of beings and their destinies such as are given in the *Kammuryō-jukyō* were probably not so much to be taken literally as representations of objective conditions, as much as they were intended to point out that any person could ultimately attain the final experience of Nirvana and enlightenment. All would depend on the devotee arousing some measure of faith and discipline to the limit of his ability. The text merely makes it clear that some persons require a longer period of religious development than others.

While the Pure Land sutras recognized a variety of religious practices, they were organized about the path to enlightenment established by Amida Buddha. In the *Muryōjukyō* itself there is the implicit rejection of other forms of Buddhism as Amida Buddha (in the person of Hōzō Bodhisattva) made a selection of all the most excellent aspects of other Buddha lands and practices.[1] As a result of this selection the way of Amida Buddha was exalted as the highest and

---

[1] Yamamoto, *op. cit.,* 16-17. Coates and Ishizuka, *op. cit.,* II, 358-359.

supreme way in Buddhism. Hence the Pure Land tradition developed a quasi-monotheistic tendency by concentrating devotion toward Amida Buddha. Shinran explicitly stated the principle in a poem:

> When we trust in the Pure Land of Amida (Buddha),
> We trust in all Buddhas.
> To praise a single Buddha singleheartedly,
> Is to praise the Unimpeded Man.[2]

In China Pure Land doctrine became more popular through the efforts of T'an-luan, Tao-ch'o and Shan-tao. In T'an-luan's teaching there appeared the tendency to view the Pure Land as a form of objective existence into which one is born at the end of life. Birth into the Pure Land was also considered the attainment of Nirvana. In mythological terms such birth came to be defined as entrance into the True Recompense Land. This sphere symbolized the enjoyment of the fruit of enlightenment and the fulfillment of his aspirations which the Buddha experienced after his arduous disciplines. This conception is related to the theory of the three bodies of the Buddha which was a basic feature of Mahayana Buddhology.[3]

In accordance with the relative values placed on the variety of modes of practice in Buddhism by the Pure Land teachers, there also grew up the theory that ways of action and belief that were not directed toward Amida Buddha or supported by the Pure Land school resulted in a birth within the sphere of the Pure Land, but not identical with the highest level. A variety of terms were employed to describe these inferior births in the *Muryōjukyō*. Some people were described as dwelling in an "Embryo Life." According to Sakyamuni Buddha's description of this state in the sutra, it is like living in a palace varying in size from fifty to a hundred yojanas;[4] a life of pleasure similar to the beings who dwell in the thirty three heavens of the gods.[5] The reason they were born there lay in the fact that these people had doubt in their minds concerning the Buddha and his wisdom. They were destined to remain in this state for five hundred years, unable to see the Buddha, hear sermons, or see the company of Bodhisattvas. The inferior births were also termed as birth in the "Palace of Doubt."[6] According to the text of the *Nyoraie* such people may be born in the embryo of a lotus where they are unable to emerge because they have not attained faith.[7] Unable to see or hear the Buddha, the individual is also said to

---

[2]*SSZ.*, II, 491. The term Unimpeded Man signifies a Buddha. Soothill and Hodous, *op. cit.*, 381b.

[3]Yamamoto, *op. cit.*, 146-147. Coates and Ishizuka, *op. cit.*, II, 197-198. *SSZ.*, II, 668.

[4]Soothill and Hodous, *op. cit.*, 197b. A Yojana is about nine English miles.

[5]Yamamoto, *op. cit.*, 68. Soothill and Hodous, *op. cit.*, 312a.

[6]Soothill and Hodous, *op. cit.*, 425b.

[7]*SSZ.*, II, 145-146.

be born in the "Border Land of the Pure Land."[8] The *Bosatsushotaigyō*, Book II, speaks of a "Land of Sloth" in which pride prevents birth into the Pure Land.[9]

The Pure Land tradition came into conflict with other schools of Buddhism on two points. In the first place, it generally regarded the True Recompense Land as the highest level of attainment in the Pure Land and virtually equivalent to Nirvana. In the second place, the Pure Land teachers insisted that the common man was eligible for birth into that land through his devoted practice of the recitation of the name of Amida Buddha.

In regard to the first point, Pure Land teachers attempted to counter the view of the more aristocratic schools such as Tendai, Zen or Shingon that the Pure Land doctrine was merely a device of the Buddha to stimulate piety among individuals incapable of performing the more rigorous and demanding disciplines of meditation and purification. They maintained that birth in the Pure Land was entrance into a transformed land and was simply a preliminary stage to the true attainment of Nirvana. Enlightenment would come only when these individuals could perform the required disciplines.

In order to illustrate the belief of the Pure Land teachers that the Pure Land was equivalent to Nirvana we can refer to Shinran's teaching on this point. In one letter he identified it with the realm of enlightenment termed the Dharma body:

> When we say that to enter the Pure Land of Bliss is to realize the Great Nirvana, or to attain the Highest Enlightenment, or to arrive at Extinction, (these terms) though differing, all refer to the gift for going to the Pure Land (Ōsō Ekō) in which Hōzō Bodhisattva transferred to us the Vow of Amida Buddha as the true cause by which we can manifest the awakening of Buddhahood which is called the Dharma Body.[10]

The Pure Land shares all the traits of Nirvana. It is infinite and incomprehensible in its nature. Shinran drew on all the traditional expressions to define the Pure Land, and therefore, it is not necessary to elaborate them at this point. In terms of the individual, birth in the Pure Land means freedom from the endless repetition of births and deaths.[11] All illusions disappear,[12] and beings, becoming as pure as the land itself,[13] achieve spiritual freedom and union with the Buddha.[14]

For the second point, Hōnen provides the clearest illustration through his interest in the common man. He believed deeply that it was the purpose of the

[8]*Ibid.*, 146. Soothill and Hodous, *op. cit.*, 474b.

[9]*SSZ.*, II, 146-147. Taneuchi, *op. cit.*, 183-184.

[10]*SSZ.*, II, 693, 505, 661.

[11]*Ibid.*, 521.

[12]*Ibid.*, 502.

[13]*Ibid.*, 503.

[14]*Ibid.*, 496-497.

Pure Land school to open the doors of the highest salvation to the ordinary person.[15]

Through their insistence on both of these points, Pure Land teachers reversed the relationship of Pure Land tradition and the Holy Path schools. On the basis that their salvation was the highest attainment and the most universal, they could claim the superiority of their doctrine over that of the Holy Path schools. Thus Shinran declared that "the excellent persons who keep the precepts of the Mahayana and Hinayana also, after they have attained true faith in the Other Power, will achieve rebirth in the True Recompensed Land, and we must know that they will not be born into the True Recompensed Land by (depending on) their preceptual virtues, various self power faiths or self power (deeds) of good."[16]

Before leaving the analysis of Pure Land destiny, we must call attention to the character of the disagreement among Buddhist schools. In general, the conception of human destiny in the Pure Land tradition and Shinran does not essentially differ from that of Buddhism as a whole. Nirvana represents the goal of bliss, freedom, or true insight within which all lesser views and means of salvation are embraced. Generally the theory set forth by Pure Land exponents was positive. Where there was competition and disagreement with other schools, there was also the tacit belief that all men, whatever their views, would eventually gain enlightenment. While there was a concern for right views, a rejection of simple indifference,[17] and a sense of urgency to accept the doctrine.[18] it was universal Buddhist principle to maintain that the compassion and wisdom of the Buddha would eventually bring all beings to enlightenment. It was further recognized that the symbols which were employed by the Buddha to encourage religious devotion in people of various capacities and inclinations had only relative truth as "means" or devices used by the Buddha in teaching. Thus disagreements, though frequently vocal and at times violent, were not as rigidly conceived as in Western religions.

Shinran followed the tradition on all the major points which we have taken up above. However, he went beyond the Pure Land tradition on two points. On the one hand, he interpreted the births into the Pure Land in relation to his view of absolute Other Power. On the other hand, he re-emphasized the aspect of altruism which had been taught by T'an-luan, but had been neglected in subsequent traditional teaching.

In respect to the first point, it has already become clear that Shinran rejected the practice of recitation as the effective means for gaining birth in the Pure Land. According to his view, the practice of recitation itself, though it is a practice devoted to Amida Buddha, also destines the individual for the Border

[15] Coates and Ishizuka, *op. cit.*, II, 188, and note page 198.

[16] *SSZ.*, II, 627.

[17] Coates and Ishizuka, *op. cit.*, III, 463-464.

[18] *SSZ.*, II, 525.

Land when it is done through self power:

> Those born reciting the (sacred) name,
> While doubting the Mystery of the Vow,
> In the palace, five hundred vain years pass.
> So (the Buddha) taught.[19]

This assertion follows from Shinran's rejection of the merit-acquiring principle in Pure Land tradition.

Further, in order to emphasize his rejection of the self power recitation in the Pure Land tradition. Shinran organized the traditional distinctions pertaining to birth in the Pure Land in correlation with his theory of turning through the three Vows.[20]

The persons who practice according to the Nineteenth Vow attain a birth described as "birth under the twin Shal trees." This birth clearly symbolizes a birth in a transformed land. The figure of the twin Shal trees refers to the trees under which Gautama Buddha passed away in India. Gautama in this Mahayana theory was a transformation or manifestation of Amida Buddha. This level of practice and destiny was regarded in this theory as a temporary or provisional path in Buddhism designed to appeal to certain types of hearers and at least arouse their desire for enlightenment.[21]

The second level of birth is the "Incomprehensible Birth" which is the result of the self power practice of recitation of the name of Buddha. Here we observe that Shinran departed from the Pure Land tradition when he depicted this birth as the result of self power recitation, because he devalued the purely physical and moralistic practice of recitation. He equated this birth with that in the "Palace of Doubt" or the "Embryo Palace."[22]

The highest level of birth is termed the "Most Incomprehensible Birth." It signifies the ultimate attainment given by faith and is the birth resulting from the absolute rejection of self power practices found either in Pure Land schools or in other paths of Buddhism.[23] The mode of rebirth taught in the *Muryōjukyō* refers to the entrance into the company of the truly assured in this life and birth ultimately in the True Recompense Land where Nirvana is experienced, according to Shinran's interpretation.[24]

In regard to the second point in which Shinran contributed to the heightening of the theological character of the Pure Land conception of destiny, we discover that he re-emphasized the aspect of altruism based on the Bodhisat-

---

[19] *Ibid.*, 485, also 611, 657, 659.

[20] See above pp. 33, 34.

[21] *SSZ.*, II, 153-154, 554-555.

[22] *Ibid.*, 156, 557-558. Because the name is recited in self power, the birth is in the Embryo palace. But since it is based on Amida Buddha's virtuous name, there is recognition of Other Power and the birth is called "Incomprehensible."

[23] *Ibid.*, 165.

[24] *Ibid.*, 551.

tva concept of Mahayana tradition.

In the course of the development of the Pure Land tradition, the evangelistic concern for winning people to adherence to the teaching, and the fact that the common people who were the object of this concern were not presumed to be skilled in philosophy or capable of understanding complicated systems of discipline, inevitably led to an emphasis on egoistic concern for self-salvation. The presentation of the way of salvation in the graphic descriptions of the hells as given by Genshin and the offer of a simple means of salvation concentrated attention on the individual and his destiny. The Pure Land tradition is notably, other-worldly in its attitude to this world, and it is predominantly individualistic in focusing on the problem of individual salvation.

Shinran is outstanding for his attempt to alter this emphasis on individual salvation. It is his concern that religion not be viewed as merely the way for people to seek their own salvation to the exclusion of other people. Here he manifests a deep insight into the nature of the Original Vow which had first been stated by T'an-luan, but which had been obscured in the popular development of Pure Land teaching. According to the Original Vow, and the Bodhisattva concept on which it is based, the Buddha declares that he would not accept or attain true enlightenment until all beings had arrived at that goal. This is a sign of the Buddha's embracing and undiscriminating compassion. For T'an-luan and Shinran, the conception implicit in the Vow makes it clear that there could be no desire for one's own salvation which was not immediately and indissolubly connected to the desire for the salvation of all men. There is a great sense of the solidarity of the saved and those to be saved which is the heart of Mahayana teaching.[25] Both T'an-luan and Shinran reject absolutely the possibility of birth in the Pure Land for one who is merely attracted to it because of its pleasures and bliss.[26] For them birth in the Pure Land and the attainment of enlightenment means a return to this world in order to seek the salvation of all beings.[27]

The historical basis for the view stated by T'an-luan and Shinran was found in the traditional Bodhisattva concept of the Mahayana tradition of Buddhism. Specifically, Vasubandhu's treatise on the Pure Land sutra organized the Bodhisattva practice into two aspects, the gate of entrance into Pure Land (Nirvana) and the gate of exit (into the garden of the defiled world). Vasubandhu showed clearly that the essence of a Bodhisattva was manifestly the desire to save others. Thus the Bodhisattva does not remain content with the bliss of the Pure Land or Nirvana, but chooses to return to the muck and mire of the sea of births to work unceasingly for the salvation of all beings. T'an-luan took up this theme in his commentary where he pointed out that the desire for enlightenment is the desire for the salvation of beings.

[25]*Ibid.*, 113-114.
[26]*Ibid.*, 114-115.
[27]*Ibid.*, 118, 488, 503, 518, 522.

In the course of the development of Pure Land teaching in its approach to the common man, the emphasis on Buddhist altruism lessened, though it did not entirely disappear. The perspective was taken that the Buddha in his all-embracing compassion had provided an easy way to the attainment of enlightenment through the practice of the recitation. Men had become too degenerate to carry out the full discipline of Buddhism. Under the influence of the concept of the degenerate age in the decline of the Dharma, altruism was not emphasized because the sense of man's sin and weakness engaged the attention of the Pure Land teachers.

The clearest evidence for the change in perspective from the more altruistic view expressed in T'an-luan to the more egocentric standpoint can be seen in Shan-tao's discussion of the meaning of the concept of transferring one's own merits and desiring rebirth in the Pure Land (Ekōhotsugan). Originally Ekōhotsugan included the aspect of a transfer of merit of the Bodhisattva to secure salvation both for himself and for others. However, in Shan-tao's story of the traveller beset by thieves it is noticeable that the theme of the attainment of *salvation for oneself* is stressed.[28]

This vivid story as we have seen previously became a standard presentation for all succeeding Pure Land teachers who employed it to typify the attitude of determination required for a person who would gain birth in the Pure Land. The story also exhibited the relationship of the teachings of the Buddhas Sakyamuni and Amida as the source of the inspiration for embarking on the dangerous journey. It was a graphic portrayal of the situation of beings in the defiled world and the way in which they are to escape. Clearly the emphasis is laid on the way of escape, the flight from the evil world to the world of bliss. The situation described acutely manifests the problem of self concern which is the basis for all religions of salvation.

In the parable of the two rivers and the white path it is striking that there is no mention of the idea of the individual returning to this world to work for the salvation of others. In Shan-tao's comment on the story brief mention is made of the idea, but it is not expanded. The emphasis on individual salvation found in Shan-tao was taken up by Hōnen as the central feature of his establishment of the Pure Land school in Japan.

Shinran opened a new emphasis on the solidarity of all beings in the attainment of salvation as a result of his own experience of sinfulness and his insight into the transfer of merit of Amida Buddha. Because he desired to reduce egocentrism in religion, he turned to the thought of Vasubandhu and T'an-luan for his explication of the significance of the Vows and the understanding of the work of a Bodhisattva. We should note in passing that Shinran's effort to reinterpret Buddhist doctrine along more altruistic lines was not permanently

---

[28]See above p.15-16. Also Zenryu Tsukamoto, *The Path of the Buddha, op. cit.,* 216-218. Also Coates and Ishizuka, *op. cit.,* III, 419-421.

successful in his own school. Rennyo's writings stress the aspect of gaining birth in the Pure Land and the expression of gratitude for being saved.

The Bodhisattva concept and the Pure Land sutras which were written on the basis of it reveal a deep concern for the spiritual plight of the masses of sentient beings. Implicit in this concern for the plight of sentient beings lies the sentiment and inspiration for a positive, outgoing ethic to alleviate the ills of mankind.

Despite the altruism involved in the ideal of the Bodhisattva identifying himself with the ills of beings in order to save them, Shinran would not permit this idea to be applied to individuals as they exist presently in the world. Men of faith are not Bodhisattvas in the flesh. One cannot consider himself a Buddha in the state of return to act for the salvation of others. The reason for this is the fact that the man of faith is not yet the man of enlightenment. So long as he is in this world in the flesh he is a passion-ridden sinner in need of help and totally incapable of helping others. He may be saved and his birth in the Pure Land absolutely assured, but, nevertheless, he is still under the sway of passion.

To emphasize his point, Shinran contrasts the form of compassion shown in the Holy Path and that of the Pure Land school. The compassion expressed by followers of the Holy Path is done through their own power and for the sake of accumulating merit for their own enlightenment. Such altruism actually enhances egoism because it relies entirely on the self for the benefit of the self. For those destined for birth in the Pure Land this view is inadequate. After birth in the Pure Land and Buddhahood is attained, it is possible to return to this sphere and work selflessly and unhindered for the salvation of beings.[29] Pure and perfect altruism is possible only when one is a Buddha, for then compassion becomes the essence of one's existence and not a means to an end.

The difficulty with Shinran's view of altruism is that it tends to make compassionate action a matter of the future and not of this world. Hence the egolessness which Shinran inculcated often took the form of a passive quietism, and when it was linked to Rennyo's ethical theory of the two forms of truth, it became an acquiescence to the reigning social mores.

Perhaps the true explanation for Shinran's attitude which prevented his taking a more positive approach to social relations was his desire to avoid the suggestion that individuals can possess the adamantine nature of a Buddha in this life. On the one hand, such a view would bring Shinran's teaching close to contemporary Tendai and Shingon mysticism. On the other hand, the impassive nature of a Buddha implied that such a being could not sin. Antinomianism was possible in the interpretation of the doctrine. His letters indicate the anxiety this caused him. He warned his followers to keep away from bad associates in their present state of existence because they might fall into evil ways.

[29]*SSZ.*, II, 775-776.

They were not to use the excuse for such associations that they were Buddhas striving for the salvation of these beings.[30]

There is, however, another aspect in which the concept of the Bodhisattvic return to this world is important in Shinran's teaching. According to him, it is possible for individuals to recognize a great teacher or benefactor such as Shōtoku Taishi and Hōnen as the manifestation of Amida Buddha in this world working for the salvation of beings. The idea of recognizing great persons as signs of the Buddha's compassion is not original with Shinran. He embraces the idea, however, to show that Amida Buddha constantly manifests himself in the historical stream so that the gospel of salvation through the Original Vow is constantly encountered. The major manifestation of this compassion in history is the Pure Land tradition itself, especially in the form of the seven patriarchs. It is for this reason that Shinran continually expresses his gratitude not only to Amida Buddha, but to Sakyamuni Buddha, Shōtoku Taishi, and all the seven teachers of India, China and Japan.

Through his teaching concerning the concept of the return of the Bodhisattva, Shinran taught that not only was religion ultimately altruistic in its essential nature, but that reality at its very heart, as represented in the Original Vow, is a reality which operates to bring beings to enlightenment despite their sin and ignorance. Compassion is the essence of religion, history and reality, and it confronts beings at every turn in great individuals, in the tradition of the Pure Land and as the name and Light from Amida Buddha which arouses the awareness of sin and the humble attitude of faith in beings.

---

[30]*Ibid.*, 692.

EPILOGUE

The course of this study has travelled through various aspects of Oriental studies, i.e., Japanese history, Chinese and Japanese Pure Land Buddhism, and the study of Shinran and his thought. We have tried to summarize the character of the transition from the age of Heian to Kamakura and to indicate the profound influence the social and political conditions of that time had on the development of Japanese Buddhism. Specifically we have called attention to the Buddhist reformers as Hōnen, Dōgen and Nichiren who, moved by the spirit of the age, shaped a new and distinctive Buddhism worthy of even more detailed study. Generally we saw that the Buddhism which they promulgated was directed at the common man in the attempt to provide him with some hope and meaning in life.

It was against this background and in this spirit that Shinran lived and taught. Born amidst the turmoil and upheaval of the demise of one age and the trauma of the birth of a new one, he was moved to manifest his disillusion and anxiety in life. Like other reformers mentioned above, he set out on the quest for spiritual insight and meaning. His disillusion, his discovery of faith, the deepening of his thought in the distant provinces as an independent teacher, and his activity as a counselor and guide for his disciples are all significant phases of his life and contribute to the formulation of his understanding of Pure Land doctrine.

We have been able to indicate Shinran's contribution to Pure Land thought by contrasting it with the tradition before him. Here we have shown that he shared the spirit of compassion toward the common man imbedded in that tradition, but yet, he transcended it by removing all legalistic aspects from it.

In order to achieve this interpretation, Shinran was in the position of at once accepting the spirit of the tradition, but denying specific ideas that made it up such as the merit-acquiring principle and the ideal of meeting the Buddha at the moment of death. This anomalous situation arose because Shinran's doctrine, though couched in traditional terms, is the outgrowth of his own inner spiritual experience. Guided by this experience, he became free of the tradition and thus able to raise it to a new level of spirituality.

In raising the Pure Land doctrine to a new level of spirituality and theological insight, Shinran was able to provide a more consistent understanding of the religious life on a more universal basis.

We have frequently pointed out that the literalistic, legalistic approach of the earlier Pure Land teachers involved them in a concept of salvation which combined the ideal of self power and Other Power. Although the earlier tradition acknowledged man's defiled state, it treated this condition abstractly rather than realistically. In actuality, the tradition was based on the Buddhist optimism that a man with earnest resolve could accumulate the merit required to purify himself from the taint of passion and ignorance. Implicit in this view is the belief that in essence man is good, possessing a latent Buddha nature which he has yet to realize. Thus the practice which the tradition prescribed for the salvation of all beings was based on the merit acquiring principle.

Shinran saw clearly, as the result of his own religious experience, the fallacy of this thought. If man is evil, he is evil, and as an evil being he cannot rid himself of his own evil nature which constitutes the very character of his being. Even the good deeds that man proposes to do all ultimately rest on evil selfish desire.

With an acute sense of human depravity, Shinran developed his theory that even faith, the will to believe, is a gift of Amida Buddha. Once this faith is aroused, salvation is assured. There need be no anxiety for the future, nor any frustrating religious disciplines calculated to close the gap between our real and ideal selves. In faith one realizes that he is a passion ridden being, dependent solely on Amida Buddha for his salvation. While such an insight might appear to some to be the death of true religion, defined as a striving for salvation, it really means the birth of a religion in which the gratification of the ego is set aside for praise of the divinity and for altruistic aspiration for all humanity. We have pointed out that Shinran rejected the concept of religion as a tool or means of gaining worldly benefit or of acquiring a future reward for oneself in some heaven. For him religious activity is the expression of gratitude to Amida Buddha and the ultimate end of religion is the salvation of all beings.

Through his interpretation of religion, Shinran permitted the defiled, evil person to accept himself as he is, regarding this condition of the recognition of defilement as the assurance of salvation. He inspired the religious life in this existence with a sense of obligation and gratitude. For him the meaning of life consists in one's gracious response to Amida Buddha's compassion in any situation in which one finds himself. The final destiny of beings is Buddhahood. Based on the understanding of what Buddhahood means, he imparted a strong sense of hope to his disciples, not an egoistic hope, but one which looked forward to the eventual realization of Buddhahood by even the lowest creatures, and in whose realization believers all share as they become Buddhas.

Thus Shinran's thought reveals itself as theologically and psychologically astute. But above all, it is evident that its great popularity rests in the meaning and hope which it offered the meanest person in the assurance of Amida Buddha's grace.

BIBLIOGRAPHY
BOOKS IN WESTERN LANGUAGES

Anesaki, Masaharu. *History of Japanese Religion.* London: Kegan, Paul, Trench, Trubner & Co., 1930. p 423.

_____. *Nichiren. The Buddhist Prophet.* Cambridge, Mass.: Harvard University Press, 1916. p. 160.

_____. *Prince Shotoku, The Sage Statesman.* Tōkyō: Boonjudo Publishing House, 1948. p. 75.

Asakawa, K. *Japan.* New York: P. F. Collier & Son, 1907-1913. p. 348.

Barth, Karl. *Church Dogmatics,* Vol. I, Part 2, The Doctrine of the Word of God. G. T. Thomson and Harold Knight (trans.), Edinburgh: T. & T. Clark, n.d.p. 905.

Buddhism and Jodo Shinshu. San Francisco: Buddhist Churches of America, Committee of Buddhist Research and Publication, 1955. p. 289.

Coates, Harper Havelock and Ryugaku Ishizuka. *Honen, The Buddhist Saint.* Kyōto: Society for the Publication of Sacred Books of the World, 1949. 5 vols. p. 955.

Conze, Edward, et al. *Buddhist Texts.* Oxford: Bruno Cassirer, 1954. p. 322.

DeBary, William Theodore (ed.), *Sources of Japanese Tradition.* New York: Columbia University Press, 1958. p. 928.

DeVisser, M. W. *Ancient Buddhism in Japan.* Leiden: E. J. Brill, 1935. 2 vols. p. 763.

Grousset, Rene. *Chinese Art and Culture.* New York: Grove Press, Inc., 1959-1961. p. 331.

Hamilton, Clarence H. *Buddhism.* New York: Liberal Arts Press, 1952. p. 189.

Humphreys, Christmas. *Buddhism.* Harmondsworth-Middlesex: Penguin Books, 1951-1952. p. 256.

_____. *The Wisdom of Buddha.* New York: Random House, 1961. p. 280.

Inagaki, Saizō. *Shinran Shōnin's Tannishō with Buddhist Psalms.* Nishinomiya, Japan: Eishinsha, 1949. p. 220

Keene, Donald. *Anthology of Japanese Literature.* New York: Grove Press, 1955. p. 442.

Living Buddhism in Japan. Bulletin of the International Institute for the Study of Religions. Vol. 6-2 (May 1959). p. 100.

Lloyd, Arthur. *The Creed of Half Japan.* New York: E. P. Dutton, 1912. p. 393.

_____. *Shinran and His Work.* Tōkyō: Kyōbunkwan, 1910. p. 182.

Masunaga, Reihō. *The Sōtō Approach to Zen.* Tōkyō: Laymen Buddhist Society Press, 1958. p. 215.

Masutani, Fumio. *A Comparative Study of Buddhism and Christianity.* Tōkyō: Young East Association, 1957. p. 184.

Morgan, Kenneth (ed.), *The Path of the Buddha.* New York: Ronald Press, 1956. p. 432

Muller, F. Max (ed.), *Sacred Books of the East,* Vol. XXI. Oxford: Clarendon Press, 1884. p. 454.

_____. *Sacred Books of the East,* Vol. XLIX. Oxford: University Press, 1927 rep. p. 208.

Murdock, James. *A History of Japan.* 2 vols. London: Kegan, Paul, Trench, Trubner & Co., 1925, pp. 667, 743.

Nakai, Gendo. *Shinran and His Religion of Pure Faith.* Kyōto: Kanao Bunendo, 1946. p. 260.

Pratt, J. B. *Pilgrimage of Buddhism.* New York: MacMillan Co., 1928. p. 758.

Reischauer, Edwin O., and John K. Fairbank. *East Asia: The Great Tradition.* Boston: Houghton-Mifflin Co., 1960. p. 739.

——————. and Joseph K. Yamagiwa. *Translations from Early Japanese Literature.* Cambridge, Mass.: Harvard University Press, 1951. p. 467.

Religious Studies in Japan. (ed.). Japanese Association for Religious Studies. Tōkyō: Maruzen Co., 1959. p. 507.

Renondeau, G. *Le Doctrine de Nichiren:* Paris: Publications du Musee Guimet, Bibliotheque d'Etudes, 1958. p. 332.

Sansom, George B. *Japan: A Short Cultural History.* New York: Appleton-Century-Crofts, Inc., 1934. p. 554.

——————. *A History of Japan to 1334.* Stanford, Calif.: Stanford University Press, 1958. p. 500.

Soothill, William Edward and Lewis Hodous. *A Dictionary of Chinese Buddhist Terms.* London: Kegan, Paul, Trench, Trubner & Co., LTD., 1937. p. 510.

Suzuki, Daisetsu T. *A Miscellany on the Shin Teaching of Buddhism.* Kyōto: Shinshū Ōtaniha Shumusho, 1949. p. 151.

——————. *Essays in Zen Buddhism.* Second Series. London: Luzac & Co., 1933. p. 326.

Takakusu, Junjiro. *Essentials of Buddhist Philosophy.* Honolulu, Hawaii: University of Hawaii, 1949. p. 221.

Takekoshi, Yosoburo. *The Economic Aspects of the History of the Civilization of Japan.* 3 vols. New York: MacMillan Co., 1930.

Thomas, Edward J. *The History of Buddhist Thought.* New York: Barnes and Noble Inc., 1933-1951. p. 316.

Utsuki, Nishu. *The Shin Sect.* Kyōto: Pub. Bureau of Buddhist Books, Hompa Honganji, 1937. p. 45.

Waley, Arthur. *The Pillow Book of Sei Shonagon.* New York: Grove Press, Inc., 1960. p. 160

——————. *The Tale of Genji,* Part 1. New York: Doubleday & Co., 1955. p. 253.

——————. *The Tale of Genji,* Part 2. New York: Doubleday & Co., 1959. p. 266.

Warner, Langdon. *The Enduring Art of Japan.* New York, Grover Press Inc., 1952. p. 113.

Watts, Alan W. *The Way of Zen.* New York: New American Library, 1959. p. 224.

Wright, Arthur F. *Buddhism in Chinese History.* Stanford, Calif.: Stanford University Press, 1959. p. 144.

Yamamoto, Kosho. *Kyogyoshinsho.* Tōkyō: Karin Bunko, n.d. p. 518.

——————. *The Private Letters of Shinran Shonin.* Tōkyō: Okazakiya Shoten. p. 115.

——————. *Shinshu Seiten.* Honolulu, Hawaii: Hompa Honganji Mission, 1955. p. 522.

Zurcher, E. *The Buddhist Conquest of China.* Leiden: E. J. Brill, 1959. p. 320.

BOOKS IN THE JAPANESE LANGUAGE

Akamatsu, Shunshu. *Kamakura Bukkyō no Kenkyū.* Kyōto: Byōrakuji Shoten, 1957. p. 355.

Fujiki, Kunihiko (ed.). *Nihon Zenshi.* III, part 2. Tōkyō: Tōkyō University Publication Society, 1959. p. 331.

Fujiwara, Ryōsetsu. *Nembutsu Shisō no Kenkyū*. Kyōto: Nagata Bunshodō, 1957. p. 318.
Fujiwara, Yusetsu. *Shinshūshi Kenkyū*. Tōkyō: Daitō Shuppansha, 1939.
Hattori, Shisō. *Shinran Nōto*. Tōkyō: Fukumura Shoten, 1950. Pp 195.
Heike Monogatari, Vol. I. Tōkyō: Fukuinkan Library of Classical Translations, Fukuinkan Shoten, 1957. Pp. 459.
Higo, Kazuo and Jirō Ōmori (eds.). *Nihon Bunkashi Kōza*, Vol. III. Tōkyō: Meiji Shoin, 1958. Pp. 412.
Hori, Ichirō. *Dengyo Daishi*. Tōkyō: Seigodo, 1943. Pp. 257.
——————. *Waga Kuni Minkan Shinkōshi no Kenkyū*. Tōkyō: Sokosha, 1955.
Ienaga, Saburō. *Chūsei Bukkyō Shisōshi Kenkyū*. Kyōto: Hōzōkan, 1955. p. 249.
——————. (ed.). *Nihon Shukyōshi Kōza,* Vol. II, Kyōto: San-ichi Shobo, 1959. p. 276.
——————. *Shinran Shōnin Gyōjitsu*. Kyōto: Hōzōkan, 1948. p. 138.
Inaba, Ensho. *Shotoku Taishi*. Kyōto: Hōzōkan, 1958. p. 339.
Inoue, Mitsusada. *Nihon Jōdokyō Seiritsushi no Kenkyū*. Tōkyō: Yamakawa Shuppansha, 1957. p. 449.
Ishida, Shigeo (ed.). *Shōtoku Taishi to Nihon Bunka*. Kyōto: Byōrakuji Shoten. n.d. p. 188.
Ishii, Kyōdo. *Senjakushū no Kenkyū*. Kyōto: Byōrakuji Shoten, 1951. p. 364.
Kaneko, Daiei (annot.). *Kyōgyōshinshō*. Tōkyō: Iwanami Bunko, 1958. p. 447.
——————. *Shōshinge Kōdoku*. Kyōto: Zenninsha, 1949. p. 307.
Karasawa, Tomitarō. *Bukkyō Kyōiku Shisō no Kenkyū*. Tōkyō: Toyokan Publishing Co., 1955. p. 607.
——————. *Shinran no Sekai*. Tōkyō: Kōbundo, 1953. p. 237.
Kasawara, Kazuo (ed.) *Shinshū Kyōdan no Tenkai*. Tōkyō: Sankibo, 1957. p. 368.
——————. *Shinran to Tōgoku Nōmin*. Tōkyō: Yamakawa Shuppansha, 1957. p. 403.
Kasuka, Murin. *Shinran Denne*. Kyōto: Shiseki Kankōkai, 1958. p. 468.
Kawakami, Seikichi. *Gutokufū*. Tōkyō: Koshindo, 1948. p. 554.
Kurata, Hyakuzō. *Hōnen to Shinran no Shinkō*. Tōkyō: Nakano Publishing Co., 1958. p. 251.
Masutani, Fumio. *Shinran, Dōgen, Nichiren*. Tōkyō: Shibundo, 1957.
Matsuno, Junkō. *Shinran*. Tōkyō: Sanseidō, 1959. p. 502.
Michibata, Ryōshu. *Chūgoku Bukkyōshi*. Kyōto: Hōzōkan, 1956. p. 304.
Miyazaki, Enjun. *Shinran to Sono Montei*. Kyōto: Nagata Bunshodo, 1956. p. 265.
——————. *Shinshū Shōshigaku no Kenkyū*. Kyōto: Nagata Bunshodo, 1949. p. 324.
Mochizuki, Shinkō. *Jōdokyōrishi*. Tōkyō: Jōdokyō Hōsha, 1922, p. 436.
Nakazawa, Kemmyo. *Shinshū Genryūshiron*. Kyōto: Hōzōkan, 1951. p. 363.
——————. *Shijō no Shinran*. Tōkyō: Bunken Shoin, 1922.
Ogasawara, Senshu. *Chūgoku Jōdokyōke no Kenkyū*. Kyōto: Byōrakuji Shoten, p. 179.
Ōhara, Shōjitsu. *Shinshū Kyōgakushi Kenkyū*. 3 vols. Kyōto: Nagata Bunshodo, 1952-1956.
Osada Tsuneo. *Shinran no Shi to Shokan*. Tōkyō: Zaike Bukkyō Kyōkai, 1956. p. 332.
Sato, Tetsuei (ed.). *Kyōgyōshinshō Senjutsu no Kenkyū*. Kyōto: Hyakkaen, 1954. p. 285.
Shinran Zenshū. 10 vols. Tōkyō: Futsūsha, 1958.
Shinshū Shōgyo Zenshō. 5 vols. Kyōto: Kōkyō Shoin, 1953.
Shinshū Yōgi. 3 vols. Kyōto: Ryūkoku Daigaku, 1928.
Tamura Encho. *Hōnen*. Tōkyō: Yoshikawa Kobunkan, 1960. p. 270.
Taneuchi, Shōjun. *Shinshū Gaiyo*. Kyōto: Hōzōkan, 1953. p. 247.

Tsuji, Zennosuke. *Nihon Bukkyōshi, Chuseihen.* I. Tōkyō: Iwanami Shoten, 1944-1955. p. 455.
_____. *Nihon Bunka to Bukkyō,* Tōkyō: Shunjusha, 1951-1957. p. 270.
Ui, Hakuju. *Bukkyō Jiten.* Tōkyō: Tōsei Shuppansha, 1938-1953. p. 1148.
Umehara, Ryūshō. Shinranden no Shomondai. Kyōto: Kenshingakuen, 1951, p. 427.

Umehara, Shinryū. *Kyōgyōshinshō Shinshaku.* Toyamaken: Senchōji Bunsho Dendōbu,
_____. *Shinran Kyōgaku.* Toyamaken: Senchōji Bunsho Dendōbu, 1952.
Yamabe, Shūgaku and Chizen Akanuma. *Kyōgyōshinshō Kōgi.* 3 vols. Kyōto: Hōzōkan, 1952.
_____. *Waga Shinran.* Tōkyō: Dai-ichi Shobe, 1941. p. 292.
Yamada, Bunsho. *Shinran to Sono Kyōdan.* Kyōto: Hōzōkan, 1948. p. 224.
Yasui, Kōdo. *Shinshū Shichisō no Kyōgi Gaiyō.* Kyōto: Hōzōkan, 1952. p. 350.

ARTICLES IN WESTERN LANGUAGES

Hanayana, Shinshō. Book Review, *The Asian Student.* 10-29 (April 7, 1962), p. 8.
Hashimoto, Hideo. "The Christian Faith and Jodo-Shin Buddhism," *Occasional Papers,* 6 (July, 1960), International Missionary Council. p. 14.
Hashimoto, Minoru. "The Keystone of Medieval Bushido," *Cultural Nippon.* IV-3, (November, 1936). pp. 263-272.
Kawakami, Tasuke. "Bushidō in its Formative Period," *Annals of the Hitotsubashi Academy.* III-1 (October, 1952). pp. 64-83.
Nanamoli, Bhikku. "The Three Refuges," *Bodhi Leaves.* Kandy, Ceylon: Buddhist Publication Society. p. 5.
Reischauer, A. K. "A Catechism of the Shin Sect." *Transactions of the Asiatic Society.* XXXVIII, part V. pp. 333-395.
_____. "Genshin's Ojoyoshu," *Transactions of the Asiatic Society of Japan.* Second Series, VII. (December, 1930). pp. 16-97.

ARTICLES IN THE JAPANESE LANGUAGE

Fujiwara, Kōshō, "In the Interpretation of the Kammuryojukyo," *Indogaku Bukkyōgaku Kenkyū.* II-1 (3), (September, 1953). pp. 171-172.
Hirose, Nanyu. "Shinran Shonin no Shusse," *Shinshū no Sekai.* II-9 (August, 1922). pp. 193-196.
Hosokawa, Gyōshin. "A Study of the Epistles of Shinran," *Indogaku Bukkyōgaku Kenkyū.* II-2, (4), (March, 1954). pp. 645-647.
_____. "A Study of the Epistles of Shinran," *Indogaku Bukkyōgaku Kenkyū.* III-1, (5), (September, 1954). pp. 203-205.
_____. "A Study of the Epistles of Shinran," *Indogaku Bukkyōgaku Kenkyū.* III-2 (6), (March, 1955). pp. 579-581.
Kaneoka, Hidetomo. "Dharani and Nembutsu," *Indogaku Bukkyōgaku Kenkyū.* II-2 (4), (March, 1954). pp. 500-501.
Matsuno, Junkō. "One Doctrinal System of Shinran's Followers," *Indogaku Bukkyōgaku Kenkyū.* III-1 (5), (September, 1954). pp. 206-209.
Miyaji, Kakue. "On Zenran's Heterodoxy," *Indogaku Bukkyōgaku Kenkyū.* IV-1 (7), (January, 1956). pp. 232-235.

Nagata, Kyōshin. "The Commentary on Singleness of Heart in the Ronchu," *Indogaku Bukkyōgaku Kenkyū*. III-2 (6), (March, 1955). pp. 532-533.

Ōchō, Ennichi. " 'Ken-i Shōnin' Theory in Jōdokyō," *Indogaku Bukkyōgaku Kenkyū*. III-2 (6), (March, 1955). pp. 617-620.

Washiyama, Jushin. "Goshōsokushū ni Shinobu Bannen no Shinran Shōnin (1)," *Ōtani Gakuhō*. XXXI-1 (February, 1952), pp. 54-62.

INDEX